"As a world traveler and writer, I often find myself struggling to accurately describe my experiences and adventures overseas. It is so hard to convey the wonderful craziness that is travel, and yet Jill has managed to do it in a way that transports the reader into her experiences with her family teaching in Guam, Africa, and Mexico, and then perfectly describes the tough transition back to 'normal' life."

    – Julie Morey, Author

Praise for *Here We Are & There We Go*

"What truly amazed me about this book was that they just jumped headlong into it with no safety net and blinders off. They made the decision to move to Guam almost on a whim. They didn't even know where Guam was. That was either very gutsy or completely crazy. And what was even more interesting was that they stuck it out, learned, and grew through it all."

– Kathleen Gamble, Author of *Expat Alien: My Global Adventures*

"Surprisingly though, I found this particular book completely fascinating. Stories of moving to unheard of islands with small children, being confronted by armed guards and dinners containing cat had me glued to the pages, and it became almost impossible to put down. Dobbe's excellent recall is an especially important factor as she gives real-life events and almost story-like quality with high levels of detail. I really liked the family unit, and it put a smile on my face to read about such an amazing family unit as opposed to cheating spouses, unrequited love, etc. As far as I am concerned, the book was over far too quickly, but I came away with a fresh look at life and feeling as though I had just travelled the world vicariously through Jill Dobbe's eyes."

– Charlotte Foreman on behalf of BestChickLit.com

"Experiencing life in many cultures isn't for everyone, but Jill's experiences of meeting celebrities like Jane Goodall and the Clintons, seeing humpback whales, learning different languages, and adapting to the most unusual customs wherever they went is like a vicarious world tour. Throughout it all, her main lesson is: 'Home is not the material place but the refuge where we spent time together.'"

– Lisa Lickel, Author

Here We Are & There We Go is a memoir of a family who is traveling around the world to work and, above all, to live. Growing up in a small town in Wisconsin, Jill Dobbe dreams of exploring the world, and marriage and children do not dampen her lust for travel. And with her cooperative husband, she fulfills her dream of traveling around the world, with two little children in tow. Working as teachers, they lived abroad and traveled to other places too. What comes out is a story that is filled with jet lag, diapers, and experiences that are sometimes funny, sometimes scary, but always entertaining. From the Pacific to Africa and back to the states, the author regales us with a story that not only crosses continents but also crosses cultures. I find Jill Dobbes' style charming and very conversational so that after reading the book, I feel as if I am talking to a good friend about her unforgettable adventures. Everyone with the itch to travel should read this book."

– Maria Beltran for Readers' Favorite

Here We Are & There We Go

Teaching & Traveling with Kids in Tow

Jill Dobbe

Ten|16
PRESS

www.ten16press.com - Waukesha, WI

FOR IAN AND ALI

While we try to teach our children all about life, our children teach us what life is all about.

~Angela Schwindt

Contents

Preface

After growing up in a small, rural town in Wisconsin, I yearned to live a life of adventure, vowing to make it a reality. Wanting a different experience from the mundane scenario of graduating from high school, getting married, and having kids, I looked forward to visiting faraway places, learning to speak different languages, and living among people of different cultures. An ordinary life wasn't for me. While in college, I traveled to Brazil, Mexico, London, and Russia, re-awakening my wanderlust. I graduated from college in May 1987 with dual degrees in sociology and education, ripe with plans to travel the world. Instead, I found myself married and pregnant with my first child.

Nevertheless, I didn't give up on my goal. Passionate, humorous, and adventurous, I knew without a doubt that my husband was my soul-mate and travel partner and we would eventually embark on that life of adventure. On our wedding day, he didn't exactly promise to show me the world; but, he did make me laugh. What better way to traverse the unknown paths of the globe than with a kindred spirit by my side?

A year later, with two young children and a curiosity to see the world, we decided to leave the United States to seek new adventures. We thought long and hard about taking our kids across the globe. We were aware of the meaningful lessons they'd acquire while exploring the world and its many cultures, but also aware of what we'd all be giving up - family celebrations, close friendships, and American amenities. Despite the planning, research, and heartfelt discussions, deep down in our heart, I knew that traveling and living abroad would be the best thing we could do for our family.

When Dan and I began our first overseas teaching posts, we instantly became part of a vast and dynamic network. While researching schools, I learned that international and American overseas schools resided in just about every country. Teachers from across the world moved to some of the remotest regions to teach. We made new acquaintances, befriending teachers from all different countries, and moved on to other locations after a few years. Such was our way of life and that of many educators living abroad. Individually, we would rack up a list of countries we lived in and regale each other with all of the places we had toured. Together we compared the schools and discussed which ones had the best financial packages, the best travel opportunities, and the best social life outside of school.

Our life of travel happened because I found a partner who shared my vision. Together, we braved endless hours on flights, acclimated to new schools, communicated in different languages, and set up numerous households. We survived the innumerable water and power outages, the hurricanes, torrential rainy seasons, and the death-defying traffic of third-world countries. All while living amongst fascinating cultures, beholding amazing sights, and reveling in once-in-a-lifetime experiences.

———— • ————

My memoir is a condensed version of my family's ten years living in Guam, Singapore, Ghana, and Mexico. It is an honest and entertaining compilation of events centered on and around a couple of American educators, who secured teaching jobs abroad and naively moved with their two young children across the world. Instead of recounting every experience and circumstance, I've chosen and detailed the most entertaining and compelling highlights that came from my memory, journal, and diary entries. I've included actual places, and with permission, the names of real people. Rather than a travel guide or reference manual, this book is an authentic and realistic look at living and working as overseas educators with children in tow. This lifestyle gave us unforgettable memories while discovering immeasurable zeal for living life as global citizens.

PART 1 – GUAM

1991-1992

Hafa Adai
("Hello" in the Chamorro Language)

Going Places

Our life as overseas educators came about after attending a weekend-long hiring fair for educators in Madison, Wisconsin. We signed up for the convention, hoping to interview for teaching positions within the state. It was not to be, though. Instead, we embarked on a very different destiny.

While observing the many schools in attendance, I noticed that Guam's public schools were also looking for teachers. I wasn't sure where Guam was or how far it was from Wisconsin, much less the United States, as I had barely heard of it. Dan was suddenly excited about living on an island, where he envisioned himself on a boat in the middle of the ocean fishing and scuba diving. So, thinking, *why not*, we interviewed and got hired. Later that evening, we drove back to our hometown and informed both sets of families that wc had just accepted teaching jobs on an island in the middle of the Pacific Ocean. After deciding to move there, we gave ourselves only four weeks to sell a house full of furnishings, pack, and get our hands on as much cash as possible.

It was a whirlwind time for all of us as we got ready for the move. There were many tears and stricken faces among our families and friends after informing them of our plan. Of course, many people thought we were nuts, and there were times when we had to agree with them! We'd often ask ourselves, *Are we doing the right thing? Are we being reckless?* However, after four weeks of yard sales, selling and storing the big stuff, moving out of our house, and packing what remained into our suitcases, we found ourselves looking forward to the adventure. Ready or not, that first overseas adventure was about to begin.

The flight to Guam took us first to LAX airport in Los Angeles, California. Not due to leave until early the next day, we stayed the night at a hotel near the airport. Keyed up and nervous about what lay ahead for us, Dan couldn't sleep and decided to take a walk. Growing up and living in a small town in Wisconsin made us naive about what can happen in a large and dangerous city like Los Angeles. He left in the middle of the night with all of our money and passports. Dan realized later he could've been robbed, murdered, or both. Our dream of living abroad could have ended that night before it began. Thankfully, he returned safely, and fate stepped in, as it did many times for us.

———— • ————

Beyond tired with two cranky kids, we finally arrived in the lush and tropical paradise of Guam. Guam, a small island and U.S. territory in the middle of the Pacific Ocean, was four-thousand miles west of Honolulu, Hawaii. Much later, I also learned it was about 210 miles southwest of the Mariana Trench, the world's deepest oceanic location. It makes me shiver even today to think that the four of us flew in a plane over those bottomless black, cold ocean depths. It was probably a good thing that I didn't know it at the time.

We arrived at the Guam International Airport in Agana during the quiet Guamanian night. Loaded down with one child and one diaper bag each, we stepped out of the plane and onto the tarmac. As we walked to the small airport terminal, the tropical heat hit us like the fiery, hot blast of a furnace. We could smell the delicious ocean air all around us and instantly felt the island's calming breezes. Even though it was the middle of the night, the day's heat still hung heavy in the air, giving us a sense of the island's usually hot and tropical climate.

"Island life, here we come!" Dan exclaimed, with a tired but hopeful smile plastered onto his face. Bogged down with luggage, I barely managed a grimace.

Eight extra-large suitcases holding half of a house worth of items surrounded the four of us as we sleepily waited inside the small airport terminal building. We hoped that someone would arrive soon to pick us up as promised. We didn't know a single soul on the island and hadn't talked with anyone from Guam since we were interviewed and hired one month earlier. Despite the belief that there couldn't possibly be many people who would volunteer to greet strangers in the middle of the night, we continued to wait with subdued excitement. Finally, and close to an hour later, we were greeted with the words, *"Hafa Adai! Hello, welcome to Guam!"* Gustavo, a tanned and heavy-set man wearing shorts and a faded Hawaiian shirt, led us out of the airport and into his car. While chatting eagerly, he drove us to a sleazy hotel on the island's northern end. Assisting Dan in lugging our bags up two flights of stairs, Gustavo opened the door to a small, dark kitchen and dirty linoleum floor. Dan dropped the suitcases at his feet and finding the bedrooms we fell onto the two beds, instantly falling into unconscious sleep.

Unfamiliar with jetlag and the time difference, Ian and Ali, woke at 2:00 a.m. ready to play. They were happy to be out of those confining airplane seats and, with their newfound freedom, ran wildly around our hotel room laughing hysterically and playing hide and seek with the now empty suitcases. Dan and I, tired and dizzy from lack of sleep, felt alone, abandoned, and somewhat bewildered about what lay ahead. Peering out through the smudged windows of our hotel room into the night's darkness, the only visible sign of activity was a fat, gray rat that scurried around the heaped garbage cans.

"Let's go sightseeing," Dan said. "We can't sleep anyway, and what else is there to do? Aren't you anxious to see what's here? Gustavo rented a car for us, and gave me the keys."

I gaped at him but then reluctantly agreed, "Okay, I guess."

Despite the very late hour, I buckled the kids and myself into the car. Dan consulted a map Gustavo had given him and drove us to the south end, where we found a long sandy beach surrounded by turquoise blue barrier reefs extending far out into the ocean. We pulled into an empty lot and stared out at the sea, listening to the waves' distant and rhythmic splashing. Dan and I wanted to live near the sea, and it was exciting to finally see the beaches where we thought we would be spending most of our free time.

However, that first trip was disheartening; broken glass and piles of garbage littered the sand everywhere. Not wanting to step over used diapers, piles of dog feces, and other miscellaneous heaps of soiled trash, we all stayed in the car. We found out later that most of Guam's beaches were too polluted to enjoy swimming in. Whenever we wanted to cool off in the water, we ended up sneaking our way into the large tourist hotels where we relished in the hotel pool and sampled the other amenities. That night, or should I say early hours of the morning, while the kids and I fell asleep, Dan tried to remain optimistic as he contemplated the upcoming weeks. Lucky for us we didn't try to get out of the car, as we found out much later that we were out at the worst and most dangerous time of the night.

There was much to see on the small island during daylight hours - rolling green hills, volcanic peaks, coconut palms, and pristine ocean views. Most of the land was uninhabited, lush, and tropical. The few roads on the south end were well-maintained and ran alongside the coastline, treating drivers and passengers to hypnotic and picturesque ocean views. As we drove along, we passed small village shops and gas stations, while meeting up with pickups and motorcycles carrying entire families. Occasionally, we'd even pass by a stray water buffalo trudging slowly along.

The Island Life

It was a scramble to find a place to live. There seemed to be a considerable housing shortage for newly-hired teachers. We found an apartment in Inarajan, a village on the southern end of the island, where Dan and I would be teaching. The small hamlet overlooked the ocean and its crystal blue reefs. It was like a postcard with tall palm trees, views of the brilliant blue waters, and cruise ships far off in the distance. Life was tranquil until rudely interrupted by the local teenagers. A favorite pastime for the teens was joyriding through the village in souped-up cars with the windows rolled down and the pounding bass of car stereos vibrating through the air. Witnessing the loud and sometimes obnoxious youths was our first indoctrination into the teenage culture of Guam.

We were fortunate to find an apartment on the second floor of a two-story cement building with an expansive driveway. Other teachers in the building were young and childless. They often spent weekends partying at the beach and scuba diving. Since we had children, our lifestyle tended to be a lot different. Our mornings started earlier, especially for our kids. Most mornings around 6:00 a.m., Ian woke up, picked up his LEGO crate, and dumped the bricks onto his bedroom's bare tiled floor. The neighbors below us never quite warmed up to our family after waking most mornings to the loud crash.

Our new apartment was unfurnished, and we continued to live out of our suitcases for the first couple of months. The day our household shipment finally arrived at our door felt like an early Christmas. All four of us stood out on our front balcony watching as the overloaded truck pulled into the driveway with our precious possessions. Besides the furniture, rugs, and clothing we shipped, I also unpacked giant-sized jars of peanut butter and mayonnaise and extra-large bags of Pampers diapers. Also, in our shipment were my six boxes of teaching materials that I convinced Dan I needed. He often complained about my many boxes and eventually threw them out in a fit of rage at the Guam post office after he was given the wrong box dimensions for our next move.

Shopping at the island's small food shops was a whole new experience; no more giant American supermarkets. There was never an abundance of food on the shelves. However, there were always varieties of items, and we could usually find everything from hotdogs to beach balls and sandals in one place. Directly across from our apartment was a small store that we often went to buy food staples, like bread and milk. Dan bounced a check there once, and we ended up paying twenty-five dollars for a gallon of milk and a loaf of bread! The owners were helpful and recognized us from our frequent visits, but still charged us an excessive amount. Dollars were the money exchange used on the island, but prices were high for everything since it all had to be shipped in, something we had never considered when planning our move.

Another time when we found ourselves low on money, Dan took a brand-new ice chest, a wedding present, out to the side of the road to sell. It was during those times that reality hit. We were alone on an island in the middle of the ocean, and we only had each other to count on. It was frightening, and we couldn't help but wonder, *"What did we do?"* Once or twice, we even resorted to calling our parents to beg for money, which put us in debt, as calling home to Wisconsin was expensive. It was an age of no computers, internet, or cell phones. Just a three-minute call to the U.S. was costly. Money also had to be wired as it took weeks, sometimes even a month, to get any mail.

On weekends we would travel to the northern part of the island to see some 'big city' life. It was home to the large tourist hotels that catered mostly to camera-toting Japanese tourists on their honeymoons or family vacations. When I needed to get to a shopping mall, I would venture to the only one on the entire island, the Micronesia Mall. It was small, but had a few stores that reminded me of home. Anderson Air Force Base, an American military operation, was also located in the north and housed air force and navy personnel and their families. The base employed many Chamorros (indigenous people of Guam) and was considered a popular tour for enlisted personnel.

The Japanese attacked Anderson Air Force Base in December 1941, just three hours after Pearl Harbor. Later, in 1972, an elderly and former World War II Japanese sergeant, Shoichi Yokoi, was found hiding in a tunnel-like underground cave on the island. When found by two Chamorro hunters, he was still healthy and even knew what the year was. He was shipped back to Japan and became a national hero. He eventually got married, ran for parliament, and wrote a best-selling book.

School Life

Our school year on the island began. My class at Inarajan Elementary School had twenty first graders. The students were predominately Guamanian, with a mix of Latino, Filipino, and Hawaiian. My classroom was spacious and had the requisite desks, chairs, and tables. It was open to the outdoors with windows on all sides. I wasn't used to the limited supplies of teaching materials available to me, though, and had to be very creative with my lessons. With no computers, the only technology available in the school was an overhead projector shared among seven teachers.

Approximately half of the teachers were locals, and the others were young teachers from the U.S. mainland. Several of them came on a one-year contract and were beginning their teaching careers. The school days were typical of those in the U.S., with students learning the same subjects. There were days when the school would lose electricity, but we carried on and taught without lights as there were plenty of windows open to the sunlight. Other days there was no water, and the administration would close the school.

Dan taught ninth-grade biology at the local high school, a short drive from the elementary school. He felt confident in teaching the local teenagers on Guam as he had experience teaching middle and high school students. Dan also worked at adolescent group homes and teen shelters, giving him experience working with challenging teens. Despite his experience and optimism, he grasped all too quickly that there would be more disciplining than teaching. The students had no interest in learning biology. Instead, his classes remained out of control, with throwing books across the classroom, screaming abusive language at one another, and lighting up cigarettes in the back of the room.

After the first few days, Dan had to force himself to go back and continue teaching. He tried multiple ways to interest his students in the subject. However, it was no use, and in one particular class, he became so enraged that he gathered up all of the student notebooks and threw them off the school balcony, where they landed in a heap in the parking lot two floors below. The next day brought no relief, and after numerous attempts to demand attention from his unruly students, Dan kicked three boys out of his classroom. When he went out to his car later that day, he noticed it had a flat tire. A thick rusty nail stuck out of his front wheel and he assumed the boys got their revenge.

It was the last straw. Angry and distraught, Dan stayed home the next three days and called the Dept. of Education, hoping to secure a different teaching position. No other vacancies existed on the island, and it was either go back and make the most of it or pack up and leave Guam. Since we had no money to spare, especially to repurchase plane tickets back to the U.S., Dan forced himself to return to the classroom and give it another try.

Dan went back to school and reluctantly carried on. Shortly after that, a colleague came to his rescue and took him under his wing, saving his sanity. Bill's advice, which Dan took to heart, was to teach what's most interesting to the students and don't rely on the textbook. With Bill's help and laid-back attitude, Dan survived the school year, and the students even started to respect him as their teacher. He no longer talked about quitting or moving back home.

Bill was a transplant from the U.S. and well-known among both the local people and the Haoles (foreigners). Bill was older and wiser and had lived on Guam for many years. Dan referred to him as an aging hippie fed up with the American way of life, who moved his family to Guam. Bill knew the culture, raised a family on Guam, and was a community member. He gave Dan tips on living with the local people, and the more we got to know him and his family, the more we started enjoying life there.

Bill became Dan's fishing buddy. Dan was impressed that Bill had built a boat, and the two spent hours on the Pacific Ocean catching tuna and mahi-mahi which is sometimes called a common dolphinfish. They even came close to a shark once. Once a month, they both called in sick to school and went fishing for the day. They'd both return the next day, exhausted and sunburned from a day out in the hot sun. The administration never seemed to catch on, or maybe they didn't mind, as Bill was a much-loved member of the faculty. It also set Dan up to face another month of teaching.

The English teacher in the classroom next to Dan's was not as fortunate. We got to know him and his wife, both teachers who came to Guam as missionaries. One afternoon Dan walked into his classroom and found the guy sitting at his desk, dazed and distressed, picking wet, grayish spitballs off his shirt and hair. The schoolroom had the distinct smell of cigarette smoke, and the floor resembled an ashtray with cigarette butts lying everywhere. It never got any better for him, and he and his wife left before the end of the school year. Dan felt bad for the guy, but didn't know how he could help him. He was happy, however, that things were looking up for him, all thanks to Bill.

Not Always Paradise

We made friends with the locals in our community and socialized with other teachers. The locals, Chamorros, were friendly with the tourists and Haoles. They loved children and lived and worked with their extended family members. The longer we were on Guam, the more it seemed that everyone was related. As the only couple with children, Ian and Ali had few playmates in our complex. Neither of them was old enough for school, and it wasn't easy finding a babysitter, or a daycare, as none existed in our area. We heard about Mattie, a small Filipino woman who raised crabs in her backyard, and after speaking with her, employed her as our sitter. Every day I'd take Ian and Ali to her house in the morning and pick them up after school. It seemed like a favorable arrangement for the first few months.

After driving to her small wooden house one day, she and the kids met me on her wide outside porch. I hugged Ian and Ali, and before leaving, Mattie informed me that she would be visiting her family in the Philippines.

She then asked, "Would you mind if we took Ian along with us?"

I looked at her with fright, "Yes, Mattie, I would mind. He can't go with you."

From then on, we were too nervous about leaving our kids with her. We didn't feel we could trust her anymore. We stopped taking them to her house, and Dan and I searched for another babysitter. We found a woman who had a small son, who was available to come to our home during the school days. It still wasn't an ideal situation, but the babysitter was a mother herself, and I felt I could trust her. Not having a daycare or reliable babysitters was one of the main reasons we left Guam after only one year. Exploring the world is one thing, but the safety of our children always came first.

———— • ————

Some days it felt like our family was living in paradise. Nature's beauty surrounded us. Our views from the steep jagged cliffs were enchanting, as many undeveloped areas still existed throughout the southern end of Guam. Driving to school each morning, I gazed out at the far-reaching and captivating Pacific Ocean. We felt fortunate to experience it all. However, the alluring and untouched land became ravaged as a hurricane ultimately hit the island hard.

Earthquakes frequently occurred on Guam, and that year we experienced our first ever. It rocked our sturdy, cement apartment building lasting only a few seconds; however, it measured 6.0 on the Richter scale. I was inside the apartment while Dan and the kids were playing ball in the parking lot. I ran out to the balcony to see what happened, as did our landlady, who lived on the bottom floor. She looked over at them, and Dan thought she was about to accuse them of making the building shake.

Months after that initial earthquake, a real disaster hit that left severe impacts on the Chamorros' lives. Super Typhoon Yuri, slammed into the island with sustained winds of up to 125 miles per hour. The damage was astronomical. Right outside of our village, the ocean waves destroyed and washed out miles of concrete roads. The roads alongside the coast became impassable for months. Vast concrete chunks cracked and broke as the hurricane winds flipped them into the air, and then dropped them yards away. Everywhere on the island, the winds wreaked havoc and tore apart homes and other dwellings.

Yuri also raged through entire cemeteries, wiping them out. Residents buried their deceased above ground, and during that night, the waves demolished the gravesites, uprooting bodies and carrying them out to sea. Days and weeks later, dead bodies washed up onto the sandy shores, not always with their heads or limbs attached.

That night, as Yuri's winds howled and the rain beat down, Dan stayed awake, sitting out on our covered balcony. He watched as the mighty winds blew lawnmowers, swing sets, and bicycles across our neighborhood. The kids and I slept through the entire storm, not waking once to Yuri's viciousness. We did, however, witness the effects of it the next day. The southern end of the island was devastated, and it took months to clean up after the typhoon. There was nowhere to drive to as roads were no longer passable. The island residents had no access to electricity and water, other than the bottled water people bought and stored before Yuri hit. We were unable to make phone calls as telephone lines were also down.

While still no running water from the faucets after five days, I was desperate to find a place to clean ourselves. Donning our swimsuits, we jumped in the car with our bath towels, bars of soap, and shampoo bottles. Dan scouted around various water inlets for places where we could bathe discreetly. Finally, we found a nearby river where other families were already washing and enjoying a swim. It looked clean and safe, and Dan pulled in next to the other parked cars.

Stopping the car, Ian and Ali climbed out. Dan joined them as they stood gazing toward the river while I gathered up our soap and towels. Together we stepped through the wild beach grass and over boulders to get to the water to bathe. I immediately took the soap and shampoo and, one-by-one, scrubbed Ian and Ali all over, getting them as clean as I could, telling them next to sit in the water and rinse off. After we all finished our baths and felt somewhat sterile and fresh, we got back into the car and set off for home; towels wrapped tightly around bodies and heads. Upon returning to our apartment, we informed our neighbors about the spot where we bathed.

"Ah, I hate to tell you," one of the guys remarked. "But that river is near a sewage dumping area, and the sewage runs straight into the water."

"Oh, yuck!" I remarked, suddenly feeling gross.

Dan and I looked at one another with grim expressions. Just the thought of sewage water clinging to our bodies was enough to send us running back to the car. Dan screeched out of the lot, and this time drove straight to the ocean. While I tried hard not to gag thinking about that stinky, slimy tainted water covering our bodies, Dan found a path to the sea, and we jumped from the car and ran in, scrubbing and disinfecting our bodies in the saltwater.

Two weeks after the hurricane, we finally got our electricity and phone service working again.

Dan telephoned our families back in Wisconsin to let them know that we survived the hurricane and were doing all right. It surprised them that such a storm hit us. They heard nothing on the news remotely concerning Guam or Typhoon Yuri. The plight of the Chamorros and the devastation of the island never even made international news. We felt even more secluded and further away from the U.S. mainland. Guam and its people seemed insignificant to the rest of the world.

Stray Cats and Stampeding Cows

Halfway through the year, we moved out of our apartment building and rented a small, newly-built house. The house, shaped like a small concrete box, was located outside of Malojloj, situated at the south end. More rural, there seemed to be plenty of animals but few people. Ian and Ali had a yard to run and play in, but half of it was jungle with banana and mango trees growing rampant, and the rest dirt and gravel. Stray cats, dogs, and even the occasional wild boar roamed nearby. Dan worried about snakes, so he brought home three fluffy yellow kittens to help with any vermin. Ian and Ali quickly adopted them as their pets; however, those sweet kitties gave Ian Cat Scratch Fever, which lay dormant until our summer vacation in Wisconsin.

Brown snakes lived on Guam, and in 2018, up to two-million roamed the island. The snakes caused extensive damage and wiped out chickens, small cats, birdlife, and other native species. Somehow, they'd also get into the wiring, which produced power outages throughout the island. Brown snakes weren't venomous, but we heard stories of them climbing up through the toilet and into baby cribs where they curled up next to their warm sleeping bodies. Lizards and geckos also ran rampant. They scurried up and down walls, ceilings, and countertops. It was my first experience with them as houseguests, but I learned to ignore them as they were adept at eating flies, spiders, and mosquitoes. The males were colorful with their bright orange and green scaly skins and beady eyes, but the poop they left behind in my kitchen was never a pleasing sight.

The island was also overwhelmed with coconut crabs, the largest terrestrial arthropod in the world. Coconut crabs could weigh over nine pounds and had massive and powerful claws that ripped open coconuts to get at the meat inside. Also known as "robber crabs," they would break into empty houses and steal shiny kitchen utensils, sometimes even shoes. They'd often sit by the side of the road, and if we'd spot one while driving, we'd make sure to swerve around it. Hitting a crab with its sharp claws could easily puncture a car tire.

After a good rain, hundreds of fat, jumbo cane toads hurried out onto the roads. There were so many that it became almost impossible to avoid them. The ugly, brownish amphibians got trapped beneath my tires, and every time I ran one over, I'd hear a distinct "pop, pop" sound and groan inwardly.

My biggest complaint with the house was the lack of air conditioning; the sun beat down on our dwelling like a square of chocolate left out in the desert. It was peaceful living in our new home, though. Traffic was almost non-existent, and we rarely heard the obnoxious car stereos that frequently reverberated through the air. Distinct sounds of cows mooing, chickens squawking, and roosters crowing broke the ever-present stillness. Never needing an alarm clock, each morning, we woke at dawn to the neighborhood roosters' shrill morning calls. We had very little shade in the yard and the afternoon's boiling sun forced us indoors. The nights were sometimes unbearable with only fans to cool us off.

One early afternoon, I joined Dan and the kids in our dirt-filled front yard. A gravel road ran directly in front of our house, but we never knew where it went or how far. It was always too hot to venture down it, and the lack of shade made it even more uninviting. Another concrete and box-like abode sat across the road from ours, and I occasionally chatted with the older woman that lived there. Roosters in large cages squawked outside her house. Her family raised them for cock-fighting, a popular and cruel form of entertainment on the island. Heeding the birds squabbling, I watched Ian and Ali kick rocks around the front yard, when suddenly; looking off into the distance, a distant roaring and rumbling grew ever louder.

"Do you hear that, Dan?" I asked, as the pulsating sounds got closer and more intense. "What is it?"

His head shot up, and he moved quickly, grasping Ian and Ali. Huddling together, we sprinted toward the house just as a thundering roar of thumping hooves pounded down the path, yards from where we stood. Roughly fifty cows barreled down that country road, kicking up dust while never veering off the dirt trail. They ran as if their lives depended on it, and as quickly as they came, they vanished. Shell-shocked, the four of us witnessed them disappear. We never saw another animal or human trek down that road again. Where the herd of cows came from, and went to, was a mystery we never solved.

Snow Comes to the Island

Dan and I spent our days teaching at our separate schools, and on the weekends, we drove to the other end of the island to shop for a week's worth of groceries and visit the beaches. The rolling hills and curvy roads often led to Ian and Ali becoming carsick. After vomiting on themselves, one after the other, Dan would stop and pull over so that we could clean them up. Their carsickness became such a frequent occurrence while driving from one end of the island to the other and I learned to expect it and made sure to bring along plenty of wet wipes and extra clothing.

On occasion, we attended one of the neighborhood fiestas. The Chamorros loved their festivals and celebrations of weddings, baptisms, and birthdays. Named after saints, the villages on Guam also held festivities to honor their saints. Pig roasts were always the main event, and people near and far were invited to participate. At our first fiesta, Ian, only two years old, nearly witnessed the gruesome and bloody killing of a pig before being roasted on the spit. Dan, in the nick of time, pulled him away before the horrific scene took place. Anyone invited to a fiesta or other gathering had better attend. Chamorros considered it rude and impolite not to show up, something I learned when our family sat one out. I didn't have a good excuse either when I was confronted about why we hadn't attended. No one ever went home early from a celebration either, as the hosts believed it to show bad manners.

The fiestas were all about eating, drinking, and dancing. Accompanied by ear-splitting music blaring from gigantic speakers set up in various locations in the yards, adults chatted while children danced. Ian and Ali joined in quickly, getting the hang of it, despite being so young. The older women who sat on the sidelines loved watching the two blond-haired Haole kids and their antics. By the time we finally arrived home, our ears rang so severely from the loud music that we could barely hear one another speak.

Food was another of the draws at these celebrations. Several long tables would be arranged end-to-end with typical Guamanian dishes such as red rice, sushi, barbecued chicken, Spam, and the centerpiece, roast pig. Hosts refilled bowls as soon as they were empty, and they never seemed to run out of food. Spam was always on the menu as it was a popular food on the island. When we first moved to Guam, a local car dealership advertised giving away a case of it with every car they sold. Dan and I couldn't help but giggle at the unusual enticement to buy a shiny new car.

On March 2, 1992, all of Guam celebrated Discovery Day, the day Magellan sailed his three ships to Umatec Village, discovering Guam in 1521. Every village celebrated with music, parades, carabao races, cockfights, and a re-enactment of Magellan's ship's mock landing.

———— • ————

Life on Guam was a continuous adventure. Our family went on never-ending trips to the ocean, where we spotted sapphire-blue starfish and floating sea anemones. Dan explored the multicolored coral off the reefs and fished whenever he could for tilapia, mahimahi, and tuna. Guam's temperatures were hot and humid, but a continual breeze blew, cooling us off most days. The rainy season began in July and continued through December, and the dry season commenced in January and went through June. The months of the dry season became unbearably hot, especially during the afternoons. Spending time outdoors was challenging as the scorching hot sun shone down from the cloudless, blue sky. Teaching in classrooms without air conditioning was incredibly arduous, and I ended most days looking like a wet rag.

Holidays were always a welcome reprieve, and since Guam is considered an "unincorporated territory" of the United States, the schools celebrated American and Chamorro holidays. Christmas was the most significant celebration with three weeks off of school. Chamorros celebrated with lights and decorated palm trees instead of the usual pines. A thin, dark-skinned Santa dropped in at the mall, and instead of his fuzzy white beard, Guamanian Santa wore brightly colored floral shorts and a Hawaiian-looking t-shirt. Snow and cold weather were unknown to our students, as most families couldn't afford to leave the island during the holiday. However, that year was the first time the snow had arrived on the island.

The day before the Christmas break, Japan Airlines filled one of its planes with ice and snow and flew it to Guam. One of the student's fathers who worked for the airlines wanted our students to enjoy a white Christmas and arranged for the shipment of snow. Much to our teachers' and students' surprise, the snow was trucked in cold storage vehicles to school and dumped in a heap near the elementary school building. Students were let out of the classrooms and shouted with joy as they jumped into the makeshift snow bank, covering themselves with the icy coldness. Teachers played along with the students on the small mountain, throwing snow at one another. I even ended up with a fist full of ice down the back of my shirt. Unfortunately, we only had forty-five minutes to play on the freezing mound before it all melted into a giant puddle of steaming water, becoming a lasting Christmas memory for all of us.

An Aussie Christmas

Foreign teachers often left the island during the Christmas vacation. That year we decided to take a once-in-a-lifetime excursion to Sydney, Australia. The day after school let out for a holiday, we boarded the plane for the six-hour trip. Despite temper tantrums and continuous efforts to entertain Ian and Ali, we forgot all about it when we finally landed in Sydney. As soon as we arrived at the Kingsford Smith Airport, we hurried through customs, hailed a taxi and drove straight to an Aussie department store. Dan and I figured we'd do a lot of walking, so one of the first things we looked for was another stroller.

We entered the large emporium, and I quickly found a sales clerk. "Excuse me. Can you tell me where I can find your strollers?" I asked.

After she gave me a quizzical look, I pointed to the one that Ali was sitting in.

"Oh, you mean a pram!" she exclaimed, and pointed us toward the second floor's escalator.

From then on, we put both prams to use, pushing Ian and Ali around Sydney Harbour, the Taronga Zoo, and along the streets of Bondi Beach.

The zoo was a big hit with so many animals to see. Even I felt excited about petting koala bears for the first time. Wallabies about the same size as Ian hopped along the paths eating out of his hands.

I nearly felt like one of the exhibits when I heard a young girl exclaim, "Mummy, they're from America!"

At the end of our Aussie vacation, my legs and arms were taut and tanned from pushing kids up and down Sydney's streets.

On our third day in Sydney, Dan and I wanted to show our children kangaroos and joeys hopping about in the wild. Dan consulted his map for an area covered by green grass, hoping we'd find a mob of Roos frolicking together. A taxi dropped us off, and we started walking along the side of the lonely road toward the grassy fields. With each child in their pram, Dan and I plodded along in a single file. A few cars drove by, leaving us in their dust, but after wandering for a good twenty minutes with no kangaroo in sight, it started to dawn on us that we might be in the wrong place to see them.

The Australian heat was intense, and our journey started to feel like a lost cause. Just when we were ready to give up, a car pulled up and stopped alongside us. The young couple was shocked to see a couple of Americans pushing two toddlers down a mostly deserted road. Rolling down their windows, they politely asked where we were going.

"We wanted to see some kangaroos in the wild," Dan and I yelled together, feeling very much like the naive Americans.

"Well, mates, you won't find any here. There aren't any kangaroos anywhere near here," the man and woman proclaimed at once, stifling giggles. "We're on our way to a barbecue for our grandmother's ninetieth birthday. Hop in and join us."

"Are you sure?" I questioned. "We have a lot of baggage."

"No worries!" they replied in typical Aussie lingo. "After the party, we'll take you back to your hotel."

After storing our prams and other baggage in the trunk, or boot as the Aussies called it, the four of us crammed into their back seat. Upon arriving at the party, we all bounded into the house where an older woman with a halo of white hair sat primly, surrounded by party guests and birthday paraphernalia. Our little family was introduced to the party goers as the Americans on a walkabout searching for kangaroos!

"Happy birthday!" Dan and I exclaimed as we stepped toward the birthday gal with Ian and Ali in tow. She smiled, her blue eyes opening wide.

"Thank you," she murmured, looking surprised but pleased to meet us. "I've never met any Americans before."

Dan and I felt like a novelty as we crashed the small birthday gathering. When Dan and Ian sat down to eat some cake, I took Ali out to the backyard. The next-door neighbor had horses, and two black and brown ponies came trotting over to the fence as we plodded outdoors. Frightening Ali, she screamed until I picked her up and took her over to pet their soft, hairy manes. We never saw kangaroos on that adventure, but we did get to pet horses and surprise an elderly lady on her ninetieth birthday.

The Sydney Zoo turned out to be the best place for Ian and Ali to frolic with kangaroos. Many of them were hopping about, and while the kids were hesitant around them at first, they got brave and trotted over to feed them bits of apples and carrots. Sydney had many peaceful parks and lush gardens, and Dan and I often freed the two from their prams, letting them race around. The numerous water fountains throughout the city were magnets to them. After many attempts to keep them dry and out of the spraying water, we finally gave in on one of our last days. It had been another scorcher of a day, and when we arrived near a bubbling water fountain enclosed by low walls, we couldn't say no anymore, and let Ian and Ali splash themselves silly. They both ended up soaking wet, but it cooled them off, and they loved every minute of it.

We spent our last couple of days at a hotel near Bondi Beach. A taxi dropped us off, and after getting settled in our room, Dan and Ali took a nap. Ian and I left the hotel to check out the beach. Holding hands, we crossed a busy street and walked over to the sandy coastline. A large concrete wall with skateboarders whisking up and down sat between the highway and the sand. As I looked out toward the ocean, I was a little shocked to notice numerous topless sunbathers enjoying the blazing hot Australian sunshine. Dan and Ali were awake when Ian and I arrived back at the hotel, hot and thirsty. While deciding where to go for dinner, I told Dan he should check out the beach the next day. However, when he returned to the waterfront that next morning it was so chilly, there wasn't a soul in sight, much less any topless action. Dan, unfortunately, missed out on the fantastic views.

Christmas week had come and gone, and despite seeing a few red decorations here and there, the Australian heat was instrumental in helping us ignore the holiday. Despite the hard work, tantrums, and diaper changes we endured while vacationing with a one and two-year-old, our trip was a memorable one. On Boxing Day, the day after Christmas, we again put Ian and Ali in their prams and walked with them up and down the historic Rocks area near Sydney Harbor. After they fell asleep, mouths gaping open, Dan and I took a respite and sat at an outdoor restaurant to enjoy the view of the Sydney Opera House while drinking a couple of Australian lagers. Sitting and relaxing in the hip, mostly tourist area gave us a chance to reminisce about the week while laughing and groaning together at the zany episodes that could only come about while traveling with two preschoolers.

Our Christmas holiday 'down under' came to an end, and we boarded our flight back to Guam. At the same time, we were waiting at the airport to catch our plane, the current U.S. president, George Bush, landed in Air Force One, but we just missed him at the airport. That night flight back to Agana occurred during a violent lightning storm that crackled and lit up the sky. Our plane shimmied and shook throughout that night, keeping Dan and I awake with terror as Ian and Ali, thankfully, slept peacefully between us. Throughout the wild flight, the plane lurched, and the sky streaked with flashes. Dan and I held hands across our children's sleeping bodies, worrying and praying almost the entire time. It was a flight from hell, and I was extremely grateful once we landed on the ground safely back on Guam.

Australia was the trip of a lifetime for us, and the longer we remained overseas, the more Dan and I were keen to visit other countries. We moved abroad to see the world, and it was our greatest ambition for ourselves and our children. While living on Guam, we experienced a multitude of emotional highs and lows. It was like living in paradise on some days, but on others, especially when we had no water or electricity, life felt primitive. Ali was still too young for school, and childcare was almost non-existent. So we started looking around for other jobs in other overseas and international schools.

Singapore and a Stop in Tokyo

After finding an advertisement for an international school in Singapore, Dan called the phone number listed. He spoke with the headmaster and learned they were hiring. They had openings for a high school science teacher and an elementary teacher, but we had to go there to interview. We had spring break coming up, a perfect time to see another country and interview, so we made reservations to fly to Singapore.

The six-hour flight on Singapore Airlines felt like a quick jaunt. Arriving at Changi Airport, we quickly hired a taxi and took it straight to the school. We showed up just to learn that the headmaster was on vacation. The high school principal heard us ask to be interviewed and brought us in. Later, she told Dan that he sounded a lot like her son, which swayed her to interview him. The meetings were brief, and we were both hired on the spot. While I filled out the massive amount of paperwork, Ali fell asleep on the high school secretary's lap. Ian found a place underneath the table and curled up to take a nap. Once we accepted the jobs and completed the paperwork, Dan and I shook the principal's hands and told her we'd be back in August.

The next day, the four of us took a ride on a Chinese junk, or boat, where we gazed out at Singapore's views from the water. We did some sightseeing in the city and took the kids to the Chinese garden. It was a hot, sunny day, and the four of us trekked around the small lakes and Chinese pagodas, admiring it all. After walking a bit around the city, we rounded a corner and stopped. Hanging from metal bars were hundreds of ornate birdcages filled with songbirds chirping and twittering. The birds' chatter turned into background music for the mostly Chinese men sitting together smoking cigarettes and drinking tea. I felt thrilled to take the plunge and relocate to Singapore; the diversity, tranquil parks, and tourist exhibits were some of the reasons we knew we'd love living there.

Set on moving to Singapore, we first had to finish the school year on Guam and resign from our positions with the Guam Department of Education. That June, a year later, we found ourselves once again selling our car and furniture, packing our suitcases, and saying good-bye to the friends we had made. When the school year ended, Dan and I longed to take a quick trip to Wisconsin for a visit after being away for eleven months. A brief stop, we left Guam in June 1992 and headed to Singapore at the beginning of August. The flight would be a long one, but when Dan made the reservations and learned we could fly through Tokyo, he thought it would be a fun break to stop there for a couple of days.

"Wouldn't Tokyo be a great place for a stopover and a nice break from flying?" I agreed, and looked forward to a Japanese stamp on our passports and another new city to explore.

We landed in Narita, Japan, after a three-hour flight from Guam. Dan and I were running on very little sleep. While packing the night before, I had absentmindedly left a bottle of liquid Children's Tylenol sitting out on the bed. I took my eye off Ian for a second, and when I looked again, he'd been holding the bottle in his hand. I couldn't be sure if he had drunk any, and he wouldn't tell me. Dan picked him up, and I plucked up Ali, and we all jumped in the car to drive to the hospital. After getting checked out, the nurses and doctors felt he didn't drink enough if any, and luckily, he didn't need to have his stomach pumped. It was our first and last visit to the hospital on Guam. After arriving back home, we put Ian and Ali to bed and finished packing. We left for the airport at 3:00 a.m.

Three-and-a-half hours later, I followed Dan through Narita International Airport in Tokyo with Ian, angry because he had to sit in his stroller, screaming at the top of his lungs. I forced myself to look straight ahead, trying not to notice the many stares directed at us. Despite Ian's red face and my bleak expression, the camera-happy Japanese pointed and snapped away on their cameras, taking photo after photo of our blonde-haired kids. Dan and I nodded at them with tight smiles on our faces while attempting to maneuver as fast as we could toward the exit and leave the airport.

Traveling around Tokyo's bustling city proved a real challenge, especially pushing both kids in strollers and lugging around multiple suitcases. After being turned away from one hotel, we redistributed our luggage, Dan carrying most of the load. Limping along for a couple of blocks, we stopped at another, just before Dan was sure his arms would fall off. He unloaded the baggage in a heap and approached the main desk, securing us a room.

On our first excursion out of the hotel, we unknowingly hit the streets during rush hour. Dressed in black, ultra-conservative suits with determined expressions plastered on their faces, the Japanese mass moved along like a murder of crows. As they speed-walked to their destinations, Dan and I found ourselves going against the foot traffic flow. Swift and agile, the business-suited Japanese swerved around our little posse of kids, strollers, and bags. It was all we could do to get out of the way of the vast stream of people and find a safe spot to figure out where we wanted to go.

Mealtimes were tricky for us. Neither Dan nor I spoke or read Japanese and found it onerous to find a restaurant. On one of our first forays to feed our hungry and whiny kids, we took a chance and chose a random place. We walked in, parked the strollers near the front door, and gathered up the kids. The small eating place was neat and clean, and the tables were low to the ground. We walked toward the center of the room and chose a table that looked big enough for all of us.

"Konnichiwa!" said the waiter, as he greeted us with a big smile.

"Konnichiwa!" Dan and I both replied, the only Japanese word we knew.

"Isn't this neat?" I asked as we each sat on one of the silk cushions that lay beside the table. Dan, at 6'4" and 210 pounds, was finding it extremely difficult to get comfortable. He tried bending his long legs so that he'd be able to squeeze under the low table and eat a meal at the same time. When his body adjusted and finally relaxed, the waiter motioned us to remove our shoes, the custom in most Japanese restaurants.

"Are you kidding me?" Dan asked as he looked up at the waiter, who didn't understand any English. "I finally got my legs arranged so that my bones wouldn't snap. How can you possibly ask me to get up again to take my shoes off?" Dan nearly cried as the smiling waiter looked on patiently.

The kids and I got up again, removed our shoes, and placed them near the door. As Dan finally unscrewed himself from his half-sitting position under the table, he looked up at me with alarm. Exclaiming in a frantic voice, he said, "Jill, I can't take my shoes off. I've been wearing the same pair of socks for three days now. They have holes in them, and they smell terrible."

I stared at him and rolled my eyes with disgust. Picking up one of the restaurant menus, I told him, "Don't bother. There's nothing on this menu that I can read, anyway. I don't even know how to order water. Let's just go."

Meanwhile, during our whispered exchange, Ian and Ali got up and started running around the tables. Laughing and shrieking, they picked up the soft cushions and swatted each other. We quickly rose, corralled both kids, grabbed our shoes, and left the restaurant in our stocking feet. Standing out on the sidewalk and attempting to stay out of the way of pedestrians, I put shoes back on the kids. Dan laced up his scuffed tennis shoes and peered up and down the street, searching for a cafe or something that looked like one. Quickly spotting what appeared to be a fast-food eatery, he pointed toward it.

"Look over there," he exclaimed happily.

There, directly across the street, stood a building with laminated pictures of American hot dogs taped to its windows. As if star-struck, Dan and I each grasped a child's hand and hurried across the busy street toward those delicious and familiar wieners and buns.

Before leaving Japan, we decided to go to Tokyo Disneyland. I was quite curious to see what a Japanese Goofy, Mickey, and Minnie Mouse would look like (no different, as we found out). We planned to take a train for the first time, and as we entered the train station, Ian adamantly refused to get into his stroller again. Dan and Ali had gotten ahead of us as I pleaded and begged Ian to sit down. My patience was wearing thin, and I started getting desperate as I knew there would be crowds of workers descending on us soon after leaving the trains. I was terrified that Ian would get trampled; he was so little. So, without waiting any longer, I pushed the stroller into him, making him cry. I then picked him up, dropped him into the stroller, and strapped him in. Not one of my more delicate parenting moments, to be sure, but I got him to the train just as the onslaught of Japanese workers rounded the corner, coming straight at us. I fought against the wave of bodies pushing the stroller forward, ignoring Ian's loud and furious outburst the entire way. Tokyo Disney looked very much like Disney World in Florida; however, we did notice that there were more adults than children lined up for rides, buying souvenirs, and shaking Mickey's hand. Except for the signs written in Japanese, it felt no different than visiting an American Disney World.

While in Tokyo, I felt a Buddhist Temple was a must-see. Consulting our Tokyo travel guide, I read up on one of the most popular and famous, the Sensoji Temple, located in the Asakusa District. A taxi dropped us off just as the skies opened up. We huddled together, trying to stay dry, but the rain started to come down in sheets. An older gentleman noticed us standing together in misery and handed his umbrella to Dan. It was his only umbrella, and he insisted that we take it. It saved us, and we were able to stay at the temple longer, even lighting a couple of incense sticks, letting Ian and Ali wave the smoke around them as other visitors were doing. Typically, when visiting another culture, most people just whisper among themselves and point at us. The kindness of the stranger impressed me, warming me to the goodness of the Japanese culture.

Those few days in Tokyo weren't nearly enough, and Dan and I hoped to return one day. "Who knows?" Dan asked. "We may also come back to teach here someday."

The Sweet and Sorrow of Reunions

Once back in Wisconsin, it felt as though we'd been gone a lifetime instead of just eleven months. We had flown to Guam the previous July, and it was now June. As a family we had missed attending a cousin's wedding, new babies, and high school graduation parties. Dan and I received the royal treatment as everyone had questions about Guam and what it was like to live there. Taking a vacation in another country was one thing, but living and working outside the U.S. was unheard of to most of our friends and family.

'What do you want to do that for?' and 'Why would you want to take your children so far away?' were just some of the questions we were asked before leaving on our overseas adventures.

I think everyone was happy to see us alive and well after embarking on such an ambitious and adventurous quest. After a few hectic weeks of visiting back and forth, living with in-laws, and trying to keep somewhat of a regular schedule for the kids, we again packed up and got ready for our next journey. However, no matter how prepared and ready we thought we were, something unforeseen always seemed to occur at the very last minute.

The night before we planned to leave, Ian came down with a red rash on his face, arms, legs, and stomach. He was listless and feverish, and we had to take him to the local hospital's emergency department. The doctor on duty diagnosed him with Cat Scratch Fever, which he had contracted from those sweet, baby kittens that he and Ali adopted and lugged around every day. Caused by bacteria called *Bartonella Henselae*, it gets into the skin through a cat bite or scratch. It's not visible in cats as they don't show any symptoms. Those cute little kittens were probably oozing with it, and we never even knew. That next morning, we headed to the small airport. Saddled with bottles of prescription medicines recommended for Ian's rash and fever, we assembled with our families in the airport lounge. Dan and I tried hard not to feel guilty as our parents hugged us all goodbye, attempting to hold back their tears.

"I feel like the worst father in the world," Dan complained as he led us toward our seats.

I felt the same. Not only were we taking our parents' very young and precious grandchildren on an airplane bound for a country on the other side of the world, but we were also leaving with a child who had a sickly-looking rash covering his body. We carried on though, and as far as

I was concerned, our journeys had just begun. There was still so much of the globe to explore and we wanted to do it while we were still young. Although it wasn't always easy with kids, and there were a few tense moments along the way, we felt that our lives would forever be richer because of our travels.

PART 2 – SINGAPORE

1992-1994

Ni Hao
("Hello" in Mandarin Chinese)

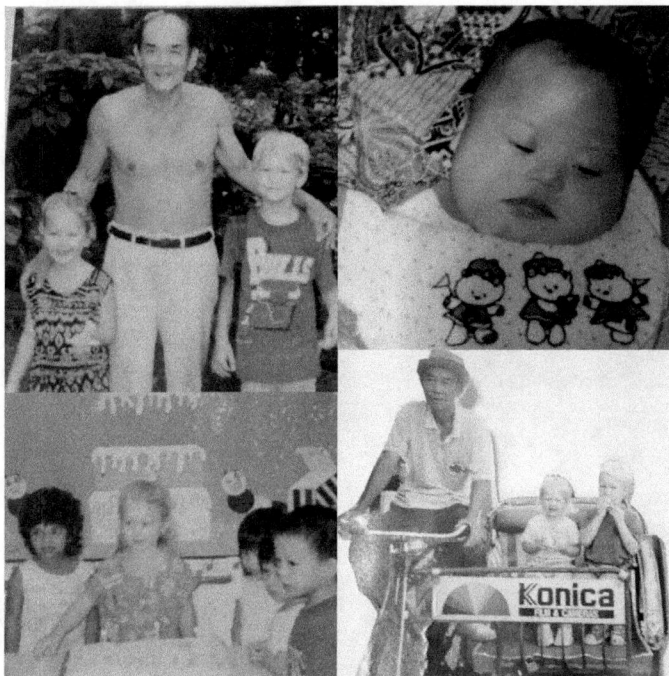

Hotels Are Homes Too

It was a long and grueling fifteen-hour flight to Singapore. What sticks out most in my mind, were the rude and cruel passengers we encountered. Dan overheard one man complain that he paid a lot of money just to have to listen to crying children. An older woman traveling with her adult daughter made it clear that she didn't want to be near any kids and hoped to have an entire row of airplane seats to herself. When she banged the armrest down on my sleeping daughter's head, I was shocked. I tried to ignore the cold looks, snide remarks, and unfriendly, scowling faces while keeping Ali happy and Ian's mind off his itchy rash. Dan and I took turns walking Ian and Ali up and down the aisles, trying to put them to sleep. It was the first of many flights when we endured Ali screaming because she didn't want to put on her seatbelt, Ian trying to make a run for it to see the pilot, and both kids attempting to use the airplane seats as trampolines. For most of the flight, it was like confining monkeys. To this day, Dan and I remember all too well what it was like flying with noisy and energetic kids, and we never complain when we have to sit next to someone else's babies or young children.

Ian's rash was almost gone by the time we arrived in Singapore. I even gave Ali another once-over to make sure that she hadn't gotten it. Once we stepped into the airport and headed to baggage claim my thoughts were consumed with making sure all of our luggage had arrived. Instead of worrying about Ian, I was apprehensive about making sure we had every piece of luggage while hoping we'd get a van large enough to transport us from the airport to the hotel.

Dan transported our suitcases onto four airport carts. While Ian and Ali clung to a handle on each cart, Dan and I wheeled them through customs. I saw the representative from the international school first, as he waved us over. The short, clean-cut Singaporean man welcomed us with a big smile, and we all shook hands. He quickly arranged for a van and sent us off to stay at the RELC Hotel on Orchard Road. The hotel became our family's home for our first week in Lion City.

By now, we had stayed in so many hotels that Ian and Ali referred to them as new 'homes.' In the course of our travels, homes became any place where we were all together. Most importantly, hotel rooms became places of refuge against the chaos of the city streets. They were locations where we spent time alone talking, playing, and relaxing. Ian especially liked taking rides in the hotel elevators and proclaimed to us that someday he wanted to be an 'elevator man.'

Singapore's sultry heat wrapped around us as our family of four wandered down Orchard Road to take in the sights. A one-way street filled with luxury hotels and distinctive restaurants, Singapore was also a shopping paradise with expensive department stores, boutiques, and shopping malls. Signs and billboards written in English and Mandarin advertised high-end items. The glitz and glamor were mind-boggling. The street was a prominent tourist attraction, and I vowed I'd be back. I already knew that living in Singapore would be incredibly different from the life we had on Guam.

After making several trips around the city looking at various flats to move to, the kids and I were so exhausted from the heat and the congested traffic that I told Dan to leave us in the hotel and go on his own. By the end of that week after visiting several places, he returned and announced he found a townhouse in Pasar Panjang.

"Where is Pasar Panjang?" I asked.

Dan replied with a shrug, "I'm not sure, but it seems like a nice area. I think you'll like it."

That weekend we were happy to move out of the RELC hotel for good.

Another New Home

Our family moved into the spacious and furnished townhouse. It included a large in-ground pool for adults and a smaller one for children. Dan, Ian, and Ali spent many afternoons in the water, where both kids learned to swim. Dan even taught Ian how to cast a fishing rod. The pools occupied the backyard, which was shared with all of the compound's residents. We rarely saw other families swimming, and happily for us had it to ourselves most of the time.

The pool, definitely the best part of our townhouse, provided our family with many hours of entertainment. The days were unceasingly hot, and swimming was the best way to cool off. Ian and Ali were like fish in the water. They loved to while away the afternoon in the water. However, much to our distress, they often missed the cues when they needed to use the bathroom. During their games of Marco Polo, neither one ever seemed to feel that they had to "go." As a result, Ian and Ali often relieved themselves right there in the pool, resulting in the gardener draining the pool water countless times.

The floor-to-ceiling glass doors off the living room overlooked a wide veranda with wicker furniture. The two bedrooms resided on the second floor, along with a sitting area. A couple of steps up from there was the master bedroom. It was over-decorated in a provocative blue velvet motif that probably dated back to the 1960s. When Dan showed it to me upon moving in, he declared how much he hated it and almost didn't rent the flat because of it.

The kitchen was the least desirable part of the house. It was minimal by Western standards but did include the requisite appliances, roughly half the American brands' size. The kitchens in Singapore tended to be smaller as it was usually the cook or maid of the house who spent time in them. During that first year, I was the only maid and cook, maneuvering myself around the tiny kitchen with no air-conditioning and minimal counter space.

While more than happy with our house and location, our next big decision was to locate a daycare for Ian and Ali. They were both too young to enroll in our school, so we had to make other arrangements. After visiting a few different nursery schools, we found the Happy Family Child Care Center clean, child-friendly, and located directly between our home and school. We visited the center, talked to the head teacher, and sat in on a few classes. The teachers spoke

English, but the students were mostly Chinese and only spoke Mandarin. We were excited about Ian and Ali learning a new language and thought the center would be perfect. Dan and I gave it a try and enrolled them.

In their charming, first-ever uniforms of white shorts and sailor shirts with blue collars for the boys and pink for the girls, we dropped Ian and Ali off the next day. Ali appeared excited when we told them they would spend the morning at the daycare; Ian seemed less sure. After the taxi dropped us off, we walked hand-in-hand down the long driveway to the entrance. One of the teachers met us at the door, and we told her we'd pick our kids up at noon. Somewhat anxious about leaving them, Dan and I kissed and hugged them, waving goodbye.

"Bye, Ian. Bye, Ali," we both shouted, as they walked inside with their teacher.

"Now, what do we do?" Dan asked me. We had a free morning and could have gone anywhere, but ended up at a coffee shop just around the corner from the daycare center.

A half-hour later, Dan asked me. "How do you think they're doing?"

"I'm sure they're fine and having fun," I replied.

"What if we just snuck over there and peeked in? We could do it without them seeing us," Dan smiled, with a hopeful look on his face. "Let's try it."

Stealthy and quietly, Dan led us towards one of the windows. We each peeked in and saw Ian and Ali playing. Ian, sensing our nearness, looked up, saw us, and started to cry. When the teacher noticed us, she came outside.

"If you come around, Ian will never get used to staying here," the teacher scolded. "You must stay away until pick-up time."

"Yes, yes, I know." Dan acquiesced, looking embarrassed.

"I told you," I admonished him as we left to buy some things for our flat.

My Introduction to Education

While our children played with their new Asian friends, Dan and I started teaching. Our school was K-12, and the student body hailed from countries all over the world. My first-grade class contained Norwegians, Irish, Indian, and Chinese students. I was no longer teaching in a solely American system like I had been in the U.S. and on Guam. I now worked alongside teachers trained in Australia, Singapore, and the UK. Working with all these diverse nationalities was one of the reasons I desired to teach abroad. Our family was now genuinely immersed in an all-embracing and global environment.

As excited as I was about the school, I soon experienced the European dislike for the American educational system. Before moving overseas, Dan and I were trained in U.S. universities and taught in the American educational system for almost five years. I entered overseas teaching, hoping to learn more ideas and different methods from my European colleagues. I admitted to learning some new and exciting ideas that I would not have come across while teaching in U.S. schools.

I never believed that the American education system was the best way to teach, nor did I feel it was the worst. However, I strongly felt that both (European and American) education systems had a lot to offer. I hoped to take advantage of both methods while teaching my classes. As one of the few American educators at the school, there were occasions during that first year in Singapore when I didn't feel wholly accepted or supported by other colleagues.

I also realized early that some British parents weren't too thrilled to have an American educator teaching their children. A British mother objected strongly to the word "period" for the mark at the end of a sentence. As a result, her son reminded me daily in his very proper English accent that it was also called a 'full stop.' It was just one of many teachable moments that year.

Exploring Singapore's Neighborhoods

Hoping to get to know some of the teachers, a group of them organized a soccer game one weekend and we decided to join. Dan agreed to be on a team, despite not having ever played the game before. I brought Ian and Ali along to watch. As one of the few teaching couples with kids, I didn't always feel a part of the young group. I chatted with a couple teachers as the kids and I watched Dan run up and down the field with the other players. When he kicked the ball into the opposing team's goal, his soccer days abruptly ended.

Later, on another sunny afternoon, while visiting an Australian family, the kids were invited to swim in their pool. As the adults chatted amongst themselves, I glanced toward the swimmers and suddenly spied poop hovering in the water. "Oh, god," I thought as I jumped up. Not wanting to bring any attention to myself, I strode over as furtively as I could, scooped it up in one hand, walked toward the bathroom, and flushed the disgusting thing down the toilet. After washing my hands for five minutes, I casually strolled back to my seat and sat down, resuming my conversation. No one said a word, not even Dan. Utterly embarrassed, I could only hope our new friends hadn't noticed.

Our family wasn't off to a very good start in our attempts to make new friendships in Singapore.

Even though my days at school were somewhat taxing, we found life in Singapore to be invigorating. No longer did we have to endure the power outages or blackouts we had on Guam. Often scorching and humid with intermittent rain, it lasted only a short time, and the brilliant sun always popped out again, drying everything up. I enjoyed the fact that I could plan activities outdoors and know the weather would be nice, unlike living in Wisconsin where it was usually cold, rainy, or snowy.

On weekends we enjoyed taking trips to the many zoos, parks, and playgrounds where local families walked, played, and picnicked. The elderly Chinese practiced their slow and methodical tai chi movements in the early mornings on the quiet grounds, while younger men and women jogged along the scenic trails. The Chinese Gardens with their oriental pagodas and exotic, multicolored flowers were a peaceful and lush oasis; however, one of our visits ended swiftly when we discovered Ian peeing on one of the fragrant patches of flowers.

Singapore had many distinct cultural neighborhoods, and we liked to explore them. While on a trip to Arab Street, Dan bought himself a sarong, which he found quite comfortable and wore around the house. Ian and Ali, with their blond locks and American accents, gained attention wherever they went. On a day trip to Little India, a tall Indian man wearing an Indian Kurta, a long shirt, plucked Ian out of my arms and walked away with him. I looked around for several panicky minutes until the man reappeared, carrying Ian with his fists full of candies.

Little India truly lived up to its name. It was probably my favorite area in Singapore. Bollywood music burst from shops selling embroidered silk saris and flashy flowered garlands. Restaurants dotted the roads saturating the air with the distinct aromas of Indian spices. I gazed around me as women in bejeweled saris crisscrossed streets and moved swiftly around intricately carved Hindu deities. I was in complete awe of everything I observed.

Months later, Dan and I made our way back to Little India. The Thaipusam Festival was taking place at the time, and I was curious to witness it. Thaipusam, I quickly learned, was an annual procession that included chanting and the beating of drums. Hindus, male and female, walked along, giving thanks, fulfilling their vows, and seeking blessings. As part of the ritual, they pierced their cheeks, tongue, face, and other body parts with sharp needles and other objects. Spectators gawked in fascination, Dan and I among them, as the devotees stumbled along in trance-like processions carrying large contraptions, known as *kavadis*, weighing up to fifteen kilograms. I couldn't help but shudder as I stared at the dedicated Hindus being half-carried along in their trances with hooks, spikes, and skewers protruding from their bodies.

When it was all over, Dan took my hand, and we strolled quickly toward the MRT, Singapore's subway train.

"I kind of feel like I'm in a trance after witnessing all that," I told Dan.

"Yeah, that was pretty crazy. I'm sure glad we didn't bring the kids," he replied.

━━━ • ━━━

Singapore was a conglomeration of ethnicities and I noticed it daily. My class of first-graders reminded me of a mini-United Nations. More than half of them spoke another language besides English and came from various countries around the world. They taught me daily about their own cultures and customs and I was always eager to learn. During International Week students paraded around the plaza in their native regalia and the mothers and nannies brought in homemade treats native to the different countries.

Dan experienced his cultural mindfulness when he started tutoring an Israeli boy on the weekends. During the tutoring sessions, he and Aaron often got into conversations about Israel. Dan also got to know his family, and they invited him to Aaron's Bar Mitzvah, which took place at one of the Jewish synagogues. A Bar Mitzvah occurs when a Jewish boy turns thirteen; it is considered his rite of passage into manhood. While growing up in Wisconsin, Dan never knowingly encountered any Israelis or attended a Bar Mitzvah. He was unsure what to expect at the ceremony. However, the family greeted him with a robe and skullcap, religious head covering, and showed him the area set aside for the men and boys. After the celebration, he congratulated Aaron, and the family told him he looked very Jewish with his beard and skullcap.

Happy Birthday Ali

Ian and Ali stayed at the daycare Mondays through Fridays. They were happy there, and we loved that they were learning and speaking some Mandarin. Ian seemed older than his classmates, mostly because he was head and shoulders taller. His height didn't seem to bother him, but he did complain that he wanted dark brown hair like all of his classmates.

He'd frequently ask me, "Why can't I have black hair like my friends? I don't want yellow hair anymore."

Ali cheerfully attended Happy Family but didn't always understand why she couldn't do what she wanted when she wanted. Often, when I came to pick her up, I had to wait patiently while her teacher spoke to her about waiting her turn.

Touching blond hair was considered lucky by the Chinese, and Ali got sick of all the hands touching her head. She turned away and scowled every time someone tried to touch a lock of her hair. It became embarrassing for us, but luckily, the Asians just laughed and thought she was adorable. The teachers also loved to squeeze and pinch her round, fat cheeks, making Ali pout even more. The childcare center was safe, healthy, and educational, and Dan and I felt very lucky to have found such a child-friendly place for our children.

———— • ————

Ali turned one in Guam and turned two-years-old in Singapore. When I addressed the head teacher about having a birthday party, she relayed that I would need to bake 40 cupcakes and bring them to the center the next day. I wasn't even sure if the oven in our apartment worked, but I had to try. I didn't want to disappoint Ali and her friends. On the day of her birthday, I awoke early and stomped down the stairs into the mini-kitchen. As I pulled out the mixing bowls, a rare thunderstorm momentarily rocked the air outside. I'd hoped it would cool off the kitchen's stifling temperature, but the sun came out again in full force. Repeatedly wiping the sweat from my eyes and forehead, I mixed ingredients and filled cupcake trays, one after the other. Over and over, I pushed trays of cupcakes into the dwarf oven and stacked the finished products wherever I found room.

By 3:30 that afternoon, I finished all forty. Dan and I hopped into a taxi, placing the plates of cupcakes on our laps, as careful as if we were transporting precious jewels. We demanded the driver hurry so that we would make it in time for the afternoon snack. The cab dropped us across the road from the building. Holding on tight to our numerous trays, we ran for the entrance and arrived just as nap time ended. Ali saw Dan carrying in the cupcakes and gave him an ear-to-ear smile. We placed them all on the table while the hungry and excited children squeezed around it. As the birthday girl, Ali stood in the center and her friends sang happy birthday to her, first in Mandarin and then in English. The teachers handed out the cupcakes, and the kids sat on the floor, eating them. Crumbs and wrappers littered the ground, and beside me, a small boy vomited his cupcake all over his uniform, letting out a lusty cry. Ali and Ian then passed out the treat bags that Dan and I hastily put together at the last minute. Ian seemed more excited about the whole birthday celebration than Ali, who soon grew tired of all the attention.

Catching a Ride

Absorbed with school and teaching during the weeks, we found little time for anything else. Each morning we took a city bus, dropping Ian and Ali at the center, hopped another bus, or flagged down one of the city's taxis to take us to our school. I preferred taking a cab as the driver always drove us straight to the top of the tall hill where the school sat; it was so much easier than trudging up that steep incline.

Public transportation was easily accessible in Singapore, so we decided to wait to buy a car. On Saturday mornings, I usually took the bus to the vegetable and flower markets to stock up on a week's worth of fruits and vegetables, like dragon fruit, mangoes, coconuts, and aubergines. The large crates overflowed with ripe and juicy fruits and vegetables in yellows, greens, and reds. I loved picking through the various fruits, some I knew, and some I didn't. I'd often sift out something unfamiliar so that the kids could experience the new and different food.

Saving the fragrant flower kiosks for last, I'd choose the brightest and healthiest fresh flowers to bring home and put in vases. Picking out flowers was always my favorite part of my shopping expeditions. I'd carry my full bags back onto the bus and ride it home, feeling a kinship with the Singaporean homemakers. I looked forward to my weekend excursions; it felt almost freeing to be out on my own in the foreign city.

Bus rides with Ian and Ali were generally entertaining. When they weren't fighting with each other, they'd often break out in songs and recite rhymes in Mandarin, their voices resonating throughout the bus. Ultimately, the stoic Chinese passengers would smile and nod at the small yellow-haired Americans. Once on a tour bus, the driver handed the microphone over to Ian and Ali. The two belted out song lyrics, entertaining the elderly Chinese riders who laughed and applauded as they listened to them recite in Mandarin. Our children with their light skin and hair always seemed to garner the Chinese's attention.

Although it was cheap transportation, riding on the bus could become long and tedious. Once on the way home, Dan accidentally fell asleep. Waking up an hour later he realized the bus had stopped, the other passengers had departed, and the driver was long gone. Still drowsy and reeling from the shock of it, Dan left the bus to search for another way home.

"Where have you been?" I asked when he finally returned home, my voice rising with concern.

"I fell asleep on the bus, and the driver never woke me up. He just left me there," Dan replied, still terribly annoyed.

Not finding it at all humorous, Dan sidled out of the room. I couldn't help but chuckle to myself at his unfortunate luck.

My own bus experience was even less comical. Needing to get to the bank on a Monday, I left school during lunch, hoping I would get there and back without any problems. I was sure it would be a quick trip, and I'd only need to take one bus to get there. I waited a short time at the bus stop down the hill from the school, and when it arrived, I promptly climbed on. Sitting and riding for a few minutes, I watched in horror as the bus turned the corner and drove in the opposite direction. Like a shot, I stood up and pressed the button. Swerving abruptly, the driver pulled over to the corner. I marched down the aisle and out the door, soon realizing I'd have to walk back to school as it was now too late to get to the bank, and I couldn't find another bus. Picking up my pace, I began to alternate between running and walking the two miles back to school, hoping I'd make it in time for classes. Cursing under my breath, I picked up my pace just as a few fat raindrops landed on my head.

More rain fell, and I arrived back at school in time to greet my students, with my clothes and hair soaking wet.

"Mrs. Dobbe, you're all wet," proclaimed a couple of astute kids. I grumbled at them and went to my desk to look for something to dry off my hair.

By the end of our first year, I no longer enjoyed riding the buses. The novelty had worn off. I resorted to taking taxis and the MRT, the best way to go when our family took more extended trips. It was clean and safe, even late at night, and I could usually manage my way around the city without getting too lost.

Red Is For Good Luck

The clamor of the cymbals and raucous thumping on the drums invaded the peacefulness of the afternoon. Concerned, I walked out the gates of our complex to check out the commotion. I gazed down the street at the musicians dressed in red while someone in a red and yellow lion costume gyrated to the clanging of gongs. A cultural performance was in full swing only a couple of blocks away.

"Ian, Ali, do you want to go watch the lion dance with me?" I shouted. "Come on. Quick!"

I took their hands, and we hurried down the street toward the commotion. Dan decided he'd seen and heard enough of the noisy displays and stayed behind. We joined the other spectators who stood on the sidewalk, watching the riotous scene. A family moved into a new house and hired raucous dancers and musicians to scare away the ghosts and evil spirits they believed still inhabited the home. Bringing good luck, joy, and happiness, the Chinese often had Lion

Dances perform at new businesses and special occasions, like Chinese New Year. Mesmerized, the three of us watched the lion dancers perform Kung Fu kicks and twist their bodies haphazardly while the musicians carried on with abandon. The enormous lion mask looked exotic, colorfully adorned in red hair, bells, tassels, and other decorations. The Chinese believed that the color red brings good fortune and wards off evil, and they displayed it everywhere. *'This continuous crashing and banging could scare away even the most stubborn ghosts,'* I thought to myself as I stood ogling the exotic performance. The blaring racket, though, hurt Ali's ears, and she covered them with both hands while we stood and watched.

On the day we visited Chinatown, it was as boisterous as I'd thought it would be. The four of us found a rickshaw and climbed in. Small and lean, the rickshaw driver jumped on his bicycle and drove us down narrow, vibrant streets decorated with red banners and lanterns. *Qipaos*, body-hugging dresses in red silk, hung outside shops. Adjacent stores displayed large slabs of meat and sea animals hanging from hooks, predatory flies clinging desperately to their slick flesh. Surrounded by tall, modern buildings, the many eateries, stalls, and shopping centers advertised their plethora of trinkets and wares while tourists and local Singaporeans jammed the streets. The historic *hutongs,* lanes or alleys separating the houses, and the two-and-three-story colonial buildings with curved roofs and splendidly maintained wooden shutters gave off an authentically oriental ambiance.

Although the kids and I treasured the rickshaw ride, it proved to be painful for Dan. Since the bicyclist was half his size, he was ready to give him a ride, getting out and pedaling the bike himself.

"I can't do this anymore. I feel sorry for the guy. I'm almost twice as big as he is. He's so skinny; he must be ready to collapse. Let's get off here," Dan asserted, clearly upset.

"Okay, let's walk for a bit," I said, lifting the kids off the wide seat while Dan thanked our tired bicyclist profusely, not minding at all when he asked for double the price he initially requested.

Most times, I found the Singaporean Chinese formal, direct, and polite. However, what continually amazed me was their extreme pushiness, especially when they had to wait for their turns in lines or queues. As westerners, we learned early on to be respectful and patient while waiting for our turns. Chinese men, especially, seemed to have great difficulty with that concept. I'd elbow Dan as we observed adults around us push their way to the front of lines, oblivious to who was around them. They didn't seem to understand the meaning of personal space either or what it meant to stand in line, as they usually stood in groups or clusters.

I always wondered if it happened to us because we were foreigners; it drove me crazy. Dan and I, observing it happen, again and again, would look at each other and roll our eyes, shaking our heads in amazement.

Grocery shopping in Singapore was never an enjoyable experience for me. Many times, while I stood in line, my arms overflowing with packaged items, I'd notice someone lurking nearby, ready to swoop in front of me. I'd glare, letting that person know I was watching, even though they usually ignored me and cut in line. On a couple of occasions, I even resorted to shouting while holding my ground.

"I'm next in the queue!" I informed that person as he stared straight ahead, pretending not to understand me.

Mr. Ho, Who?

"Ni Hao Ma!" Every morning, in their newly acquired Mandarin, Ian and Ali greeted our kind, old gardener.

"Hao!" he'd reply, smiling down at them.

Despite a melting-pot of cultures and languages, English was still widely spoken throughout the country. The locals also communicated in *Singlish*, a blend of Malay, Mandarin, Hokkien, Cantonese, and English. The slang word, 'lah,' was widespread and often used at the ends of sentences, sort of like a verbal exclamation point. It's also the most widely used Singlish term. We heard "ok, lah" often and began to use it ourselves. We quickly picked up British vocabulary, too. Trucks became lorries, elevators were now lifts, car trunks were boots, and the bathroom was the loo or only the toilet. When Ian started first grade at our school, he started calling me "mum," sounding a lot like his British classmates.

The Singaporean Chinese accent was difficult to decipher at times. Hand gestures and facial expressions came in handy when we were face to face, but telephone conversations could be challenging. On one occasion, the phone rang, and Dan answered it.

"Hello?" Dan retorted.

"Hello, this is Mr. Ho," the man replied.

"Who?" Dan asked.

"Ho," the caller responded again.

"Who?" Dan questioned him again, confused.

The conversation continued in that vein for a good five minutes—"Ho." "Who?" "Ho." "Who?"—I never learned if the conversation went beyond that, but Dan eventually figured out that the man's name was Mr. Ho. Ho was a popular and common surname in Singapore.

Our times eating out in Singapore were always an adventure with international cuisine in abundance. The hawker stalls were popular open-air food courts with copious stands featuring Indian, Malay, Chinese, and Indonesian food. The booths lined the complexes, and entire families filled the plastic tables and chairs nightly. Despite their popularity, occasional bouts of food poisoning resulted from, among other things, unrefrigerated food left out in the hot weather too long. We learned of a young boy the same age as Ian, who ate dinner at a hawker stall with his family and became gravely ill with a severe stomach ache, passing away the next day.

Dan and I also had a favorite Mexican restaurant. It was the only Mexican eatery we found in the city, and we went there as often as we could for date nights. Another favorite, especially with Ian and Ali, was Bugis Street, an outdoor area once favored by tourists and transsexuals. Its flamboyant heyday took place from the 1950s to the 1980s, but was more family-oriented by the time we visited. Our kids especially liked it because of the enormous aquariums that held octopuses, lobsters, fish, and crabs. Dan and I could always sit and enjoy a leisurely meal while the riveting sea creatures entertained our kids.

Dinnertime for our family was usually around 5:00 p.m., another reason our family stood out as foreigners. We often surprised waiters when we'd sit down and ask for menus.

Looking at us oddly, they'd ask, "Why are you eating so early?"

Growing up in large families in mid-western Wisconsin, everyone ate dinner at five or six o'clock in the evening. That time stuck with us, even though Singaporeans often ate much later. Having kids with early bedtimes also made it virtually impossible to eat an evening meal any later.

I'm mindful of healthy eating, and I dutifully read the Happy Family Center's menu so that I'd know what Ian and Ali were consuming for lunch each day. However, some of the items served sounded almost inedible, with fish balls, eel skin crisps, and fish head soup on the menu. Ian and

Ali never complained about the food, though, and I was just happy I no longer had to scour the market shelves for lunch items that would please their American taste buds. Thankfully, they weren't picky eaters, as I could never find Skippy Peanut Butter or Kraft Mac n' Cheese anywhere in the markets.

———— • ————

After several months of living in Singapore, I developed an ugly, itchy red inflammation on my legs and arms. Once a month, I walked to the allergist's office to receive an injection of an antibiotic. The rash cleared up, but like clockwork, it came back a month later, and off I would go again to get my monthly jab. The shot worked so well that I wasn't even embarrassed about dropping my pants and getting it in my derriere. Singapore was the only place where I acquired those welts. I didn't know if it was from the food I was eating, dust particles hanging in the air from all the building construction or if it was the hot, humid air that caused them, but I was miserable. After leaving Singapore, the skin rashes never bothered me again.

Contraband and Caning

My days at school were stressful, however, the students, minus a couple of rowdy boys, were lovely. Their parents were supportive; even the British mother seemed to accept me finally. Some British and Australian teachers were very aloof, unfriendly, and downright hostile. I lost weight that first year and developed a sinus infection that took me out of school for a few days. One of the kindergarten teachers who lived in our complex eventually warmed up to me. Her husband also taught at the school, and our daughters started to play together. Our friendship progressed, which helped somewhat to reduce my feelings of inadequacy at the school.

Overall, the school was a happy place, and most days, I was thrilled to be there teaching children from different backgrounds and cultures who played and worked together. There were no racist attitudes among the students, and they accepted one another unconditionally. It had always been my hope that Ian and Ali would grow up culturally aware, living in a community that included people of all races, colors, and religions.

It turned out that Singapore, with its extreme diversity, was a perfect place for that.

Dan had mostly positive interactions at the high school and fit in well with his worldly colleagues. He found his high school students' antics amusing and often relayed their comical acts to me. In one such account, while on hallway duty, watching students come and go, he noticed a boy lurking in the hallway during his rounds. The student carried a leather briefcase instead of the usual backpacks. Curious, Dan sidled up to him and asked to see inside the case. The boy shifted closer to the hall lockers, with Dan at his side. Carefully unlocking the case, the high-schooler revealed his voluminous stash of gum packets in a variety of colors and flavors. Apparently, he was known around the school as the 'gum dealer.' Dan couldn't help chuckling about the student's lucrative side-business.

Months later, the police arrested a student in one of Dan's classes. The Hong Kong boy and an American student from another school spray painted a fleet of parked luxury cars and stole road signs. The Singaporean police found both boys and sentenced them to a caning, the form of corporal punishment still used in Singapore. Both boys received a sentence of eight to thirteen smacks on the rear end with a bamboo cane. Days later, Dan's student returned to school, giving him and the class a detailed account of the experience. The boy claimed it hurt for about five days to sit down.

Caning is the punishment meted out for many offenses; vandalism and overstaying a visa are just two of them. Before the caning occurs, male inmates strip naked, and the doctor examines them, deciding whether or not they can withstand the caning. Prison officials then confer with the doctor about the number of canings to be given. While the inmates› bare backsides are openly displayed, the jailers fasten the wrists and ankles to the «caning trestle,» and the beatings begin.

Singapore, a city-state, is well-known for its safety and cleanliness. The streets are empty of trash. Spitting on the streets is forbidden. Anyone caught chewing gum or disposing it in a public place could incur a severe fine, community service, or a public caning. Stores aren't allowed to sell chewing gum, and tourists can only bring up to two packs per person into the country. On a more frightening note, any drugs brought into Singapore are automatic death sentences for those individuals.

Santa Dan

When December approached, we prepared to spend Christmas in Singapore. Dan and I wanted to make it memorable for Ian and Ali since they wouldn't celebrate with their grandmas and grandpa in Wisconsin. When one of the pre-school teachers asked Dan to play Santa Claus, I piped up and immediately volunteered him.

"Mr. Dan?" she asked. "We need a Santa Claus. Would you be interested?"

"Yes, yes!" I immediately shouted. "He'd love to do it!"

Dan, realizing he had no choice, took the costume. Days later, and despite what felt like the hottest day yet, he donned the decadent red suit, furry hat, and fluffy white beard. Driving to the center, already sweating, he cranked up the air conditioner, and cold air filled the car. Dan parked our vehicle out of sight so that Ian and Ali wouldn't notice it, and the two of us jumped out.

Jolly old Santa Dan showed up at the daycare, shouting, "Ho! Ho! Ho," carrying a huge sack over his shoulder, filled with gifts for all the kids. The children watched with wide-eyed innocence as Santa Claus bounded into the building. Surrounding him, forty eager and curious dark-haired Asians and two yellow-haired foreigners clamored for his attention. Caught up in the noise and excitement of Santa Dan's arrival, a few tried to climb up onto his lap and pull off his beard. Dan bellowed a few more "Ho-Ho-Ho's," all the while disguising his voice so that he wouldn't give himself away to Ian or Ali. I stood outside the melee and snapped photos of the kids and Santa. Ian and Ali seemed none the wiser that their dad was the man behind the bushy beard. After an hour in the stifling suit, Dan, sweating profusely, had to leave. Making his way out the door, he hollered, "Merry Christmas" one final time.

That night we asked Ian about Santa's visit to the center. Ian piped up, "Santa Claus was wearing the same ring as you, Dad."

Ian didn't say anything else about Santa's visit, which made us wonder if he knew it was Dan or not?

Our festive mood continued, and we decided to hold a Christmas party in our townhouse. A true multicultural celebration, we invited the daycare teachers, parents of Ali and Ian's Indian and Singaporean friends, and our British, American, and Australian colleagues and neighbors. I planned, baked, and decorated traditional American Christmas cookies and candies while sweating in my stuffy kitchen.

Almost everyone we invited showed up. The kids hustled upstairs to play while the adults chatted, ate, and drank downstairs. We could hear their shrieks and laughter and didn't see any of them the entire night.

Later in the evening, a crowd of carolers showed up, and we invited them in. What felt like, an entire church congregation filled up our living room, dining room, and stairway as we joined them in singing Christmas songs. After the singing stopped, the carolers swooped down on the drinks and snacks and soon mingled with the other guests. Not long after, their chatting turned religious, and as the evening winded down and the carolers moved toward the door, one of my colleagues leaned over and whispered to me, "I think Jesus has just saved me."

———— • ————

When March rolled around that year, the entire school participated in "Classrooms Without Walls." Middle and high school teachers and students traveled to other countries for a week, while elementary school teachers planned activities around a particular theme. That year, Dan chaperoned fourteen Japanese students, eleven females and three males, and flew to Kenya in East Africa. On the way to Kenya, they made a stop on Mauritius Island, climbed Mt. Kenya, camped under the stars, visited the indigenous Maasai tribe, and traveled in a safari across the Serengeti Plains.

Dan arrived home with photos and souvenirs. He traded his baseball cap for a batik wall hanging and a couple of pairs of socks for a *rungu*, a massive wooden throwing club used by the tribe to knock out goats and other animals. The wall hanging still hangs on my wall at home, and Dan always packs the club in his suitcase, bringing it along on our travels. Thankfully, though, he's never had to use it for protection or for killing any meat.

Along with gifts for his family, Dan relayed his favorite story from the trip. After his group arrived at a campsite, where they were to spend the night, he helped the students get settled and pitch their tents. While everyone was busy, a small monkey wandered over and tried to snatch food or anything else it could get its hands on. Being the man-in-charge, Dan defended his campers and picked up a large stick to scare away the monkey. Raising it high in the air, he took several steps toward the baboon and proceeded to frighten it away. The thief ran into the jungle, and the students congratulated Dan on his heroics until the monkey returned, waving his own more massive stick. Upon noticing the students' stricken faces, Dan turned around, saw the monkey, and yelled for everyone to run inside their tents.

Summertime Travels and High Teas

Toward the end of the school year, Dan and I decided not to fly home for the summer vacation. Instead, we taught summer school and bought a family car. Dan purchased the little red European vehicle from another expatriate and was the sole driver. It didn't take long for him to conquer driving on the right-hand side of the road, and soon we were taking trips all over the island, even into neighboring Malaysia. I was always too nervous about attempting to drive in the speedy traffic and on the opposite side of the road, even though Dan was still willing to teach me.

Weekend getaways from Singapore were easy and cheap. Committed as we were to visiting as many new places as we could while overseas; Dan and I would look for travel opportunities which were only a short flight from Singapore. On one long weekend in June, the four of us flew to Phuket, Thailand. Unfortunately, it rained almost the entire time; however, Ian and Ali still had a ball running on the sand along the ocean. Sometimes, we found ourselves strolling through the town as early as 7:00 a.m., passing by dolled-up drag queens, black eyeliner smudging their eyes as they slumped home sleepy-eyed after their long all-nighters.

Weeks later, after summer school ended, our family traveled to Bali, Indonesia. After a nine-hour flight, we arrived in Kuta, a hustling tourist mecca, left the airport, and immediately rented a jeep for twenty dollars a day. With Ian and Ali buckled into the backseat, we set off the next morning to explore as much of the island as possible. Dan studied a map of the island and headed east. We drove to the Sacred Monkey Forest, where the kids delighted in watching monkeys scurry around. Ubud, a quaint hamlet known for its culture and arts, was our next destination. While spending a few days in the hilly and picturesque town, we listened to storytellers and marveled at the Balinese dancers in their elaborate costumes and exquisite eye makeup. The four of us wandered through the scenic town and stopped for chicken satay and fried rice at the small cafes. The community artisans, pedaling their wares, spotted us right away, hoping to entice us into purchasing their crafts.

After leaving Ubud, we drove into the highlands of Mt. Batur. The kids were hungry, so we pulled into a hilltop restaurant where we indulged in the most delicious banana pancakes I've ever tasted. A demure Balinese man, wearing a colorful *udeng,* the traditional headdress of

Balinese men, sat cross-legged outside the diner playing an instrument that looked like a bamboo xylophone. He motioned for both kids to sit with him while he plunked on the keys. When he asked to read Ali's palm, though, she stubbornly refused and placed her hands behind her back.

Taking Dan's palm into his gnarled, lined hands, he announced, "You will live to be an old man."

"Oh, good," Dan replied, looking pleased.

The sweet Balinese man next took mine and pronounced, "You will make a great deal of money in sales."

After gazing hard at Ian's flat palms, he exclaimed to me, "Your hands are identical, so whenever you tell him to do something, he will probably do the opposite."

"That explains why I can't ever get him to do what I say," I declared to Dan.

Trekking Mt. Batur would have been too strenuous for our two-and- three-year-old's, so after getting our fortunes told, we drove on to the village of Tenganan. Considered one of Bali's oldest and most remote settlements, entering it felt like I was going back in time. Only the Bali Aga people, those born in Tenganan, are allowed to actually reside in the village. The four of us stepped through an entrance in the stone wall which surrounded the community. Strolling along the rocky paths, we swerved around the cows and goats that grazed between the family dwellings. The ancient stone structures and lack of motorized vehicles gave the village a primitive and timeworn aura.

Appearing to be the only tourists in sight, the residents of Tenganan eyed us curiously, while young and old villagers peered out from their darkened doorways. The residents we did come across seemed hesitant and shy, and the entire place was eerily still and quiet. I did, however, find an open shop and stepped inside. Woven cloth in subdued tones hung outside. Immediately drawn to the exceptional weavings, I approached the young man in the shop and asked about them.

"This is the sacred *geringsing* cloth that we dye and weave in our village. The women weave them on back-strap looms and wear the cloth during our festivals," the Balinese man explained.

"The colors are beautiful," I remarked while he pulled out a variety of fabrics in muted shades of reds, browns, blues, and violets. I oohed and aahed at the fine spun *ikat* weavings, fingering one after another. I chose a few fabrics and bought them, knowing they'd look ideal on my walls in Singapore. I knew that my geringsing cloth would someday bring back unforgettable memories for me of the ancient village of Tenganan and the magical island of Bali.

Earlier in the trip, Dan bought a CD of wooden flute music. It became our soundtrack for the entire drive through Bali. As we drove back to Kuta one final time, we listened to the soothing sounds of flutes and reminisced while Ian and Ali slept in the backseat. On the way to the airport, we again passed by mesmerizing scenes of ancient plows working in the rice fields and women in batik sarongs walking on the sides of the road, baskets of fruit balanced on their heads. Children with comical smiles on their faces ran toward us in bare feet, shouting and waving two-finger peace signs.

Singapore hotels held British high teas with champagne brunches on Sundays. Upon arriving back in Singapore, colleagues from school invited Dan and I out to one of them. *A perfect way to spend a Sunday*, I thought. The hotel had a playroom for the kids where they could also eat and watch movies. We dropped them off, and Dan and I spent two hours indulging in adult conversation, an excellent buffet, and all the champagne we could drink. After our boozy lunch, we picked up our two tired and cranky kids and drove them back home.

After dropping Ian and Ali off with the babysitter, Dan and I returned to the hotel to attend the Persian carpet auction going on. We sat on folding chairs and watched as the auctioneers held up hand-knotted carpets in every color from Iran, Afghanistan, Pakistan, China, India, and Russia. Silk and wool rugs covered the walls and floors. Still feeling good from all of the champagne he drank at the brunch, Dan continually raised his hand to bid for rugs. We ended up taking home five carpets that day, one in silk, all in reddish tones, and some room-size and smaller. Rolled up and tied, we squeezed each one into our small red car and drove home with the lot. The rugs overlaid every inch of available floor space in our living and dining rooms.

Months later when we left Singapore and arrived at the airport, Dan acted as nervous as a drug dealer. Since the U.S. government banned anyone from bringing Persian rugs into the U.S., he was sure the dogs would sniff ours out, or he would be stopped and questioned. Our suitcases were bulging at the seams with the ten rugs we eventually acquired. Under the guise that we were tourists on our way back home from a lengthy vacation, we sailed through customs without a hitch. Our carpets made it to Wisconsin without being seized, and they continue to lay on my floors today.

The trip to Bali turned out to be just the family adventure we'd needed - a new culture, lush scenery, and unusual sites. We returned to Singapore with renewed anticipation and foresight for the school year. Before the first week began, our family took a quick day trip to Sentosa Island, a popular resort with Singaporeans and tourists. We rode the MRT and stopped across the island. From there, we took a monorail and got off. Surveying the grounds and overcome by the sheer numbers of children and adults, I hung on tight to Ian and Ali's hands. The four of us gawked at the hordes of small dark-haired children running amok while their parents chased them from one attraction to the other. It turned out to be a long and exhausting day. By the time we entered our house, we were ready for the vacation to be over and school to start.

Chloe

Ian started kindergarten at the start of our second year in Singapore. His classroom was across from mine, and I loved seeing him engage with his classmates. Again, he was one of the tallest children in the class, this time, though, he wasn't the only American. Ian quickly latched onto the other American boy, and they became fast friends. Year two at the international school became a little more relaxed and less stressful for me. I was familiar with the elementary school, I knew more of the parents, and I had a good relationship with the principal. Despite some lingering animosity from a teacher or two, I started to feel optimistic, like I finally belonged.

Things were looking up, and life, in general, was going smoothly. At least we thought so. Castenia, a preschool teacher at the center, surprised Dan and I when she announced her engagement, especially because she wanted Ian and Ali to be in her wedding party. I was thrilled; however, Dan was not. He didn't like that our children were to be the token "white kids." The Happy Family center, where the bride and groom held the service, was transformed from a daycare center into a fairytale land. Decorated with white flowers and ribbons, the room and special raised altar gleamed. The bride and groom's families filled up most of the seats, but I found two empty chairs for Dan and me in the front row where we'd have a good view of our kids.

Dressed as a miniature bride and groom, Ian in a little boy's black suit and bowtie, and Ali in a white, fluffy lace dress, took their roles very seriously. As they moved at a snail's pace down the aisle, each child gave us a little grin before walking up to the altar and standing side-by-side directly behind the couple. The longer the ceremony dragged on, the more I worried about Ali. After fifteen minutes, I noticed that she was already starting to fidget, having had enough of all the wedding fuss. I prayed my willful three-year-old would be able to last.

"Oh, no," I uttered to Dan. "She's going to bolt if the service doesn't end soon."

"I'm afraid she's going to jump off the altar and run outside," Dan murmured, staring at Ali.

Thankfully both kids held up until the end. A crowd of Asian women surrounded and fawned all over them as soon as they jumped down from the altar. I safely moved them toward where Dan was seated. I handed them each a piece of the wedding cake, and after gobbling it up, we congratulated Castenia and her new husband and left for home to jump into the pool.

———— • ————

A little while after the wedding, our lives changed remarkably. On occasion, Dan and I talked about overseas adoption, but decided to put it off into the future and wait for the right time. But, when a neighbor dropped by and informed us of a newborn baby that needed a home, we thought that maybe now was the time. The one-week-old baby girl was being cared for by nuns at a home for unwed mothers. One of the teenaged mother's gave birth and abandoned her. The sisters who lived there weren't able to care for the baby indefinitely, either. Without many details and the vaguest of directions, the four of us drove to the place where we hoped to meet with the nuns now caring for the infant.

Almost immediately after arriving, I held the newborn in my arms. She was such a tiny bundle, weighing only five pounds. The baby was Chinese with black eyes and delicate wisps of dark hair. It was also apparent from her almond-shaped eyes and flat face that she was born with Down Syndrome. Despite it, I fell in love immediately and wanted to bring her into our family.

"Can we take her home with us now?" Dan asked the sister. Without any hesitation or even a reference check, she said yes. The nuns gathered up her blankets, diapers, clothes, and bottles, put them in a cardboard box, and handed them to Dan. We left there, now a family of five. While driving on the highway headed back home, we came up with different names, finally deciding on Chloe Ngiam, keeping her Chinese surname.

After bringing Chloe home and getting her settled, we enthusiastically embarked on getting all the supplies needed for a newborn baby. We virtually had nothing. I sent Dan out to the local market to buy formula, along with more diapers and bottles. We bought and borrowed baby furniture and clothing. In just a matter of days, we had acquired a third child. I soon realized we needed extra help.

On Sunday after Chloe arrived, Dan hurried off to a hotel on Orchard Road where they were holding a 'nanny round-up.' We needed to find someone to stay with Chloe during the day while we were at school, so off Dan went to interview nannies. It was a whirlwind of questioning, and he came back home, tired and exasperated.

"There were too many girls, and I couldn't remember one from the other. I had no idea who to hire," he explained to me when he got home.

Dan eventually hired Joy, a sweet, young, and petite Filipino woman who cared for our children until the day we left Singapore for good. Hiring a live-in helper was new to us. Many foreign and Chinese families in Singapore hired young women from the Philippines, Malaysia, Indonesia, and other countries to care for their children, often leaving their own families behind to make money. The Chinese were often the hardest on their nannies. We heard stories of live-in help forced to reside in closets, work seven days a week, morning to night, with no time off, even getting beaten by their employers.

Soon after bringing Chloe into our home, we attended meetings for adoptive parents and consulted an attorney to start the adoption process. Chloe went for medical check-ups, and we waited anxiously for the three-week exam that would tell us the condition of her heart. Ali stopped attending the daycare center, and Joy took care of her and Chloe during the days. Upon arriving home from school in the afternoon, I took over, feeding Chloe, changing her, and cuddling with her. She rarely cried, and we were hopeful that she was getting healthier every day. Sadly, however, Chloe never made it to her three-week doctor appointment. She passed away in her sleep one night, and I found her cold and blue in her crib the next morning.

Devastated upon seeing her lifeless body in the crib, I screamed for Dan. He raced into the room, picked her up, and wrapped her in a blanket. I followed him out the door with Ian and Ali. We drove to the nearest hospital's emergency room, where she was taken from us and immediately pronounced dead. The four of us said our goodbyes to Chloe as she lay on the examining table, a tiny bundle asleep. Back home hours later, adding to our distress, the local Singaporean police came to check out the incident. Three uniformed policemen entered our home, climbed the stairs to the bedroom, looked around, and left, telling us nothing. The official death notice stated Chloe passed away from complex congenital heart disease brought on by Down Syndrome. The autopsy also indicated she had a large hole in her weak heart.

Dan and I stayed home from school the next day. Still utterly distraught, we made arrangements for Chloe to be cremated and picked out a gray cylindrical marble urn and cover for her ashes. Making our way to the city morgue for a final and brief glimpse of our baby, I endured a sight of Singapore I had never wanted to see. Families all around us openly sobbed and wept as their loved ones were wheeled out on tables, uncovered, and then quickly taken away. After twenty minutes, an attendant in a white coat brought out Chloe in such a rapid manner I almost missed her. Looking from Chloe to me, Dan shouted in anguish at the man, but he had already taken her inside.

On a brilliant, sun-filled day, our neighbors accompanied our family to the crematorium.

Before Chloe's body entered the cremation chamber, Ian and Ali placed her dolls and animals beside her.

"She will want them in heaven, mommy," Ali reminded me.

We held a small memorial service in our living room on the weekend after the funeral, attended by friends and neighbors. Large standing bouquets sent by school administrators, colleagues, and our families from abroad, filled our home and terrace. A colleague read aloud the book, *Old Turtle* by Douglas Wood, a classic and spiritual fable given to our kids as a gift from Dan's mother. The message, the interconnectedness of all beings, gave us hope that Chloe would always remain a part of our family.

On many days after Chloe left us, I found myself inconsolable. The pain was always at the surface. While at school, or home, I'd find myself suddenly losing control, sobs bursting forth. Ian and Ali, still so young, called Chloe their angel in heaven. At times, I wondered if the young mother who gave birth to Chloe had learned of her passing. We never heard from her, but a nun from the unwed mother's home visited us to offer her condolences. I remember breaking down in her presence, in such pain that I could barely talk to her. She even offered to let us adopt another baby at the time, but we were still too raw with grief to consider it.

———— • ————

The school year soon came to an end, and with it, our teaching contracts. Still grieving, we decided to return to Wisconsin. Our contracts didn't allow for a large shipment back home, so I decided to sell what we couldn't take with us. Our neighbors from the complex, mostly Chinese, descended upon our house, grabbing whatever they could carry while negotiating with me over the smallest amounts. Dan and I packed up what was left, including Chloe's stroller and the urn containing her ashes. I couldn't bear to leave her in Singapore, knowing she'd be so far away from the only family that loved her. With heavy hearts, we said our goodbyes to Singapore that June 1994 and carried with us all of the memories our family had created during those years.

By now, Ian and Ali were seasoned travelers and looked forward to flying over the ocean once again. Hanging on tight to my carry-on that held the fragile urn, we arrived in Wisconsin amidst the warm sunshine of a summer day. After the two years in Singapore, life in our hometown felt discordant. Dan and I now had to readjust to life in the U.S. Fast-food eateries were everywhere. And we couldn't help noticing how overweight many people were, compared to the lithe Singaporeans. Reverse culture shock set in.

After reconnecting with our families, buying a car, and moving to a new home, we settled into daily life. I kept thinking, though, that something was missing. My head and body were in Wisconsin, but my heart was somewhere else. I couldn't help feeling disillusioned that my dream of living overseas had come to such an abrupt end. The niggling voice inside me would not let go until I found a way to get us back overseas again.

That year in Wisconsin, Dan got a job as a temporary teacher and I homeschooled Ian and Ali. I also filled my days calling schools and pursuing teacher want ads in international publications. I contacted friends still living and working abroad, and Dan and I attended a recruiting fair in Iowa. Not wanting to give up on my dream, I remained focused and determined. I resolved to continue our foreign adventures, and by July 1995, our family was on the way to Ghana, West Africa. It was to be our most extended stay and one of our most rewarding cultural experiences.

PART 3 – GHANA, WEST AFRICA

1995-2000

Akwaaba
("Welcome" in the Twi Dialect)

Obruni

Africa is a continent that I never considered journeying to, much less living. On the day I came across the school's advertisement for teachers, I excitedly asked Dan, "Have you ever heard of Ghana in West Africa?" He replied he hadn't but told me to go ahead and give them a call. Six months later, we arrived in Accra, the capital, where another kind of culture shock rocked our family.

Here we go again, I thought to myself as the airplane hit the runway with relative ease. Passengers clapped as the plane came to a final halt. Glancing over at Dan, I smiled, jittery with the realization that we had just flown five thousand, seven hundred miles to West Africa.

The four of us gathered our carry-on luggage and followed the other passengers off the KLM plane. Ian, six years old, and Ali, now five, seemed well-rested and much more alert than Dan and I after the twenty-hour flight from Chicago to Amsterdam and onto Ghana. A little more independent now; their temper tantrums were mostly a thing of the past. Together, we stepped into the small terminal of Kotoka International Airport, and advanced toward the customs lines. Clutching all four passports in his fist, Dan waited restlessly for the agent to call our family to the counter. Moments before our official entry into Ghana, I heard someone call out our names, *Hello, Dobbe's*!

Waving frantically at us was Marjorie, the American School superintendent and our new boss. A few months prior, she had flown to our hometown in Wisconsin, interviewed Dan and me in a double-occupancy room at a four-star hotel, and hired us. Seeing her again brought up a myriad of emotions—anxiety, uncertainty, apprehension—all of those internal feelings I'd struggled with before another big move. Breaking out in unexpected tears, I hugged Marjorie, and then quickly wiped them away, composing myself, lest anyone think I was unbalanced. Despite my anxious feelings, our family was about to embark on a life-altering adventure.

Hustling out of the airport into the oppressive night, Ian and Ali clung desperately to the carts spilling over with our hulking bags. Marjorie led us out of the airport toward the parking lot, where Ghanaian men swarmed us like lions to their prey, eagerly pushing and shoving their way toward us. Clutching Ian and Ali to me, I watched the mob scene unfold. The men crowded around, hoping to earn a few Ghanaian *cedis*.

Nervous and agitated at their intrusiveness, Dan tried desperately to maneuver me, himself, our kids, and all of our belongings toward the school van. His temper flaring, he shouted, "No, I've got this. I don't need your help! No! No!"

Reaching the van, Marjorie quickly introduced us to Sylvanus, the driver. We all said hello before we jumped in, slamming the doors behind us. While a small gathering of disorderly men stared, Dan and Sylvanus hastily stowed the luggage and hopped in after us. Dan let out a huge sigh and wiped his sweaty forehead.

"Wow, that was hectic," he stammered. "Is it always like this?"

"Yes, I believe so," answered Marjorie.

Sylvanus drove the van out of the airport parking lot and into the city of Accra. Dazed and shell-shocked, we stared out of the windows into the darkness. Pitch black with sporadic pinpoints of light glowing in the distance, Accra looked uninhabited.

While driving on, the van's headlights cast an eerie glow, and fiery sparks from burning candles and cooking fires flickered in the night. Sylvanus turned onto a dirt road, and we bumped along until stopping at a massive gate. He tooted the horn twice, and the gate opened with a loud scraping noise. Driving into the yard of our new home, Sylvanus braked on a large cement slab. As I jumped out of the van, the fragrant aromas of wood smoke and lemons assaulted my nose, making me sneeze.

While difficult to detect in the blackness, our house appeared to be a large, pastel green, one-story concrete building with a flat tin roof. Marjorie ushered us through the floor-to-ceiling glass doors, where we gingerly stepped into a vast living area. I immediately surveyed the room, noticing its sparseness. A lone couch and a couple of cushioned chairs sat in the very middle of the room.

"I was so happy to find matching furniture for you," Marjorie stated, looking pleased with herself, while Dan and I stared open-mouthed at the uncomfortable and hideous-looking living room set.

Once Marjorie left and we sat on the chairs, our initial reactions remained the same. The cushions were rock-hard, and the attached headrests poked out so far that after sitting against them for only a few seconds, our spines felt misaligned. We never told Marjorie how much we hated the furniture, deciding instead to keep it in another room and never use it. Long and narrow, the kitchen had plenty of cupboard space, an American-sized stove, and a refrigerator already stocked with eggs, bread, milk, and juice. A clay water jug sat near the sink, something we desperately needed since we couldn't drink the water until it was boiled first and then poured through the purifier. A long hallway with windows covering an entire wall ran through the house. A T.V. room and three bedrooms lined the hallway.

On our first night in the house, Ian, Ali, and I slept together on one bed, locking ourselves in the room for the night. Dan, however, stayed awake. Upset over the lack of good locks on the doors and the many curtain-less windows, he stayed up all night roaming from one room to the other. With his Maasi club in hand (the same one he bartered his socks for in Kenya), he spent the entire night watching and listening for thieves to break in.

Waking up to the sound of roosters crowing, as we did each morning on Guam, I felt curious and anxious to explore our new neighborhood. The four of us dressed quickly and ventured out of the gate. The intoxicating smells of animal dung and raw sewage permeated the air as we strolled down the dirt lane. Dodging holes along the way, we chuckled as frisky goats brayed and scampered out of our way. A young man in frayed shorts and a t-shirt two sizes too small walked past us carrying a wooden shoeshine box. The sights and sounds, so different from anything we'd experienced thus far, simultaneously thrilled and frightened us. I zigzagged down the road, avoiding piles of animal excrement, while women in bright orange, green, and blue batik clothing passed by on their way to the communal water pump. With their babies strapped to their backs, the sturdy females walked, purposely balancing pails of water on their heads. Gazing at them, I couldn't help but notice their immaculately rigid postures. Their bra-less, nursing breasts sagged, but their stances remained beautifully erect.

Making our way back to the closed gate, we stood outside for a few seconds wondering how to open it. Suddenly, with a loud *screech,* it swung free. Holding onto the heavy door was Peter, our day guard, and gardener.

"*Akwaaba,* master," he announced in a high-pitched voice while straining to hold the heavy door open for us.

Standing at 5'4" and weighing 140 pounds, he didn't look very menacing for a security guard. His high-pitched voice was difficult to understand, but he spoke English, so we chatted a bit, to get to know him. We learned that he lived in the servant's quarters behind the house and slept on the cement floor with bits of rags covering him. Peter told us he had been anxiously waiting for our arrival as he had no money and hadn't eaten since the last tenants moved out. We never asked him how long ago that was, deeming his plight too awful to comprehend fully.

Despite his small stature, we looked to him for help and safety as we settled into our new home and life in Accra. Dan gave him money to eat and told him to buy himself a mattress while also giving him the job of finding a locksmith to come to our house and put locks on all the doors. We needed to know that our home was safe so that Dan could get a good night's sleep and not worry about thieves.

"Yes, master, I will go and come," Peter acknowledged, wasting no time.

Besides the constant pruning and weeding in our yard, Peter ran errands for us and fetched soccer balls for Ian when he kicked them over the fence. He took all of his jobs seriously and came across as responsible and hard-working, proving himself indispensable. However, the one thing that Dan could never get him to do was to call him by his first name.

"Call me Dan," he told Peter.

"Yes, master," Peter answered.

Then Dan, "No, please, call me DAN."

"OK, master," Peter said again.

"NO, CALL ME, DAN!"

"Yes, master."

And over and over, it would go until Dan finally gave up and accepted being called master. He found it uncomfortable at first but soon got used to it, even suggesting teasingly that I also rcfer to him as the master.

The locksmith arrived and installed the locks. Once we completed that household task, we needed to find curtains or window coverings. Every room in our house had tall windows, and we wanted them covered, away from the curious eyes that always seemed to follow us. Dan and I explained to Peter what we wanted, and he arranged a taxi for us, taking us to an area of the city where batik cloth was designed and dyed. The driver dropped us off next to an open-air shed where men and women worked alongside large vats of dye. I sauntered over to the extensive tables eyeing the workers as they stamped designs made of wax onto huge cotton fabric pieces. The wax blocks the pigment from parts of the cloth, making elaborate designs. After the patterns cover the fabric, the entire material gets submerged into barrels of green, blue, orange, and black dye. After all of the water is rung out, the cloth is laid out onto the ground to dry. I moved over to view the many fabric pieces already drying in the sun, choosing to buy a couple of blue and green textiles. A woman picked them up and took them over to the wide tables for ironing. Hot coals heated the heavy iron and I waited for her to finish. Once the cloth was flattened and bundled together, Dan paid and we jumped back into the taxi for home. After finding a seamstress to make curtains out of the fabric, we hung them over the windows. The drapes didn't match any furnishings, but they did brighten up the drab rooms.

———————•————————

Getting around Ghana was relatively easy. Taxis were abundant but weren't very comfortable with their torn vinyl seats, defective doors, and the occasional hole in the floor. Before we acquired a car, taxi drivers drove us everywhere we wanted to go. Tro-tros, or mini-vans, were also cheap and popular transportation. They made frequent stops letting people on and off. Often filled to bursting, passengers hung out of windows and off the sides. Riders piled the roofs with boxes, suitcases, baskets of food, caged chickens, and even goats, securely tied.

Drivers could buy everything from toilet paper, key rings, sunglasses, gum, paintings, and Kleenex packets on the streets. As soon as cars stopped at a red light, sellers descended upon them to display their merchandise. Bedraggled kids, holding spray bottles and rags at the ready, popped out prepared to wash windshields for a few cedis. Beggars were also out, but giving them money encouraged the practice to continue. We had so much, and many Ghanaians had so little. Once, while waiting for a red light, a naked man jumped in front of our car.

"Is that man . . . naked?" I asked Dan in disbelief.

"Yeah, I think so," he muttered. "Don't look at him."

Shocked but finding it hard to look away from the indecent sight, Dan quickly rolled his window down a crack and slid a few cedis toward the deranged man.

"Please use this money to buy some clothes," he shouted at him while hurriedly rolling the window back up and driving off.

The Ghanaians we met were helpful and friendly. When we'd ask them for directions, they'd often give us wrong information, rather than not help at all. Ghanaians had the whitest teeth and the brightest smiles. They called us *obruni*, or white people, and accepted us with warmth. *Akwaaba*, or welcome in the Akan language, was the greeting they used most often to show their hospitality. A sign with the message is even displayed at Kotoka International Airport to welcome newly-arrived visitors to Ghana. Dan started practicing the special handshake that Ghanaian men used. It began by grasping hands in a typical handshake. As the hands pulled away, they twisted and snapped each other's middle fingers, making a sharp sound when done correctly. He used it often and quickly got the hang of it.

Where the Winds Blow

The school term began three weeks after our arrival. Ali started kindergarten that first year and Ian, first grade. He was again the tallest student in the class, but not the only American. Students from all parts of the world filled their classrooms. Dan and I were part of a varied teaching staff that included educators from Canada, Europe, New Zealand, the U.S., and Ghana. The entire school was small and had a homey atmosphere. Happily, for us, the administration hired other overseas couples with kids, and the local teachers also had children who attended the school. Our family didn't feel so different anymore. To kick off the new school year and welcome us to Ghana, the U.S. Ambassador invited the American teachers to his residence for an evening fete. While there, we met Edward Brynn, his wife, and his son. Throughout the night, we mingled, chatted, and ate hors d'oeuvres. Later in the evening, Ambassador Brynn showed us the piano that was still in occupancy from the time Shirley Temple Black was in residence as the U.S. Ambassador to Ghana.

Daily life was slow and relaxed in Accra, due mainly to the severe hot and muggy weather. With the ever-present heat and humidity came lethargy. By the end of a school day, we were always exhausted and only wanted to escape the heat and the blazing sun. Our classrooms were not air-conditioned, and as soon as we fled the school and arrived home, I rushed into my room to cool off under the air conditioner. It wasn't unusual to go to the shops, kiosks, or even government offices during the middle of the day and witness employees sound asleep, their heads resting on desks or countertops. Even a couple of hours of shopping on the weekends, going from shop to shop while buying bread at the French bakery, choosing different cuts at the meat market, and purchasing staples at the grocery store, would drain us of energy and wipe us out for the rest of the day.

The harmattan winds that the local teachers warned us about came early to Ghana during our first year. Sand blew through the levered windows that never closed tightly, leaving the house covered in a thick layer of dust and sand. The dust made us sneeze, and grit stuck to our teeth. When those Sahara winds blew, the visibility was so minimal it felt like living on Mars. Like a hut on the beach, dirt, dust, and sand blew inside our home. It took a lot of dusting and sweeping to keep the large house sand-free, so I hired a maid.

Sarah was a godsend who came to us from a missionary family that moved back to the U.S. She spoke English well and had family living in northern Ghana. Sarah stayed with us during the entire five years we lived in Accra, becoming part of our family. She cleaned and mopped the floors, dusted the furniture, and kept the house as sand-free as possible. Thanks to Sarah, I never had to do any housework during all those years. It was common for Ghanaian men to have more than one wife, and because Sarah was a constant in our house, Dan often joked that she was his 'second wife.'

I bought my family's food for the week and always bought fresh, so every Saturday, I'd go off to the outdoor markets to shop for fruits and vegetables. Stout Ghanaian homemakers in their vibrantly colored clothing sat guarding piles of bananas, tomatoes, papaya, and jackfruit, eagerly waiting for buyers.

"Akwaaba," the market ladies beckoned me over, offering a taste of their ripe produce, wheeling and dealing with me on the prices. Dan often came along and joked with the market ladies, making them laugh while giving us a few extra papayas, bananas, or mangoes for free. After we finished shopping, we'd transport it home to Sarah, who'd clean and soak the fruits and vegetables in water, bleach, or iodine until they were hygienic enough for us to eat.

Sarah loved to cook and bake American dishes, and, knowing English, she was able to read the recipes I gave her. Ghanaian foods took a lot of time to prepare and cook, compared to American dishes. They overused palm oil in their cooking, and when baking a cake, they never used less than a dozen eggs. *Fufu*, made from mashed yams, cassava, plantains, and *banku*, were just some of their staple dishes. Banku, a fermented corn dish, gave off such a sickening smell when cooking that only our family dogs enjoyed the food. *Kelewele*, Ghana's version of fast food, was a mouth-watering dish of ripe plantain with a combination of spices, ginger, chili, and cloves, all fried in hot oil. Our family's one favorite was *Jollof* rice, a spicy dish that included meat and tomato sauce. Ghanaians also ate plenty of goat meat and chicken dishes, but any other animal meat was circumspect. Even Marjorie, the school superintendent, was unknowingly served cat-meat at a party once.

———— • ————

Dan realized soon after moving into our house that Peter couldn't be our sole security during the days and nights, so we employed two more guards, one for the evenings and one for the weekends. It was typical for households to have guards to protect the outside property.

Instead of guns, they carried whistles and blew them to frighten away anyone who tried to enter guarded properties. The personal guards, maids, cooks, and nannies weren't always to be trusted, though. Aware of the employer's routines and habits, fired workers often came back to rob the house. Word got around of particular families waking up in the morning to find their entire house ransacked. We never considered firing any of our household help. Sarah and the guards needed their jobs, and we made sure to pay them well for their loyalty.

Isaac, a boxer by day and our guard at night, often fell asleep on the job. Dan occasionally checked on him in the middle of the night and found him snoring and slumped over in his chair numerous times.

"Isaac, Isaac! Wake up!" he'd shout in his ear to rouse him.

"Sorry, sorry, master," Isaac would wake and attempt to pry his eyes open.

"I need you to stay awake all night," Dan sternly told him, watching to make sure that Isaac got off his chair and wandered around the house and yard.

A high concrete wall covered in bits of jagged glass ran around our vast yard. It separated our back garden from an overgrown jungle where we imagined all kinds of poisonous animals roamed freely. Ian and Dan, curious about the dense, swampy area, peered over the tall barrier one morning, instantly spotting a spitting cobra sitting upright in the tall grass.

"Isaac!" they immediately hollered. "A snake! Hurry!"

Isaac sprinted toward them, clasping his foot-long, blow-dart gun. Standing next to Ian, he held the hole of his dart gun up to his mouth. In one quick, hard blow, the dart shot out, making a direct hit to the cobra's head. The snake toppled into the grass.

"Oh, my gosh!" Dan hooted and hollered with excitement after the cobra fell to its death.

"Wow!" Ian, in awe of Isaac's incredible dart-blowing skills, exclaimed incredulously. "You're my hero!"

School, Snakes and Soccer

During our second year, Dan moved to middle and high school as the science teacher. Fearful of snakes, he wasn't too happy to learn he inherited a python as part of his science classroom. The former science teacher left behind a live python snake in a glass cage, becoming Dan's responsibility. The snake, appropriately named Monty Python, measured five feet and survived on one live rat, or if there were no rats, two live mice, per month. Pythons are known to eat an entire rodent very slowly over a long period. When feeding time came around, Dan invited my class of second graders to watch the event. I found it somewhat gruesome, but the students loved it. Despite being Monty's caretaker, Dan never got used to dropping live mice into its cage, waiting for the snake to gulp them down. He eventually had Monty taken out into the wild and let go.

———— • ————

Our weekdays started early with the thwacking sounds of Peter 'mowing' our grass with long blades. Waking before the others, I packed lunches for the four of us, as the school had no cafeteria or vending machines. Before we left the house, Dan doled out malaria medicine for each of us. Ian didn't like swallowing pills and gagged and cried before finally getting them down. I looked on helplessly as Dan, frustrated, urged him on. Once Ian finally choked them down, we bolted for the car, a gray Nissan, given to us by the school. Dan put in a Smash Mouth cassette, and we rode to school listening to *Then the Morning Comes.*

The American school, located in the village of Dzorwulu, was only a ten-minute drive from our house. Each morning we crossed a busy highway where local school children wearing brown and yellow uniforms, school bags swinging on their backs, walked briskly to their schools. Before driving onto the school grounds, we'd avert our eyes from the men unzipping and relieving themselves at various spots along our route. It took a while to get used to those sights. However, it didn't take long to become desensitized to the views of men, women, and children shamelessly urinating and defecating along the roads, near buildings, or anywhere outdoors.

Dan maneuvered the car into the gravel parking lot. Kicking up loose gravel, he'd angle for a spot under the large shade tree with leaves the size of pizza pans. Gathering up homework, school bags, and lunches, we'd climb out of the car and scamper off to our separate classrooms. Leticia, a first-grade teacher and life-long friend whose classroom was next door to mine, always arrived before us. Her oldest son was the same age and in the same class as Ian, and our families often got together on the weekends.

Along with our kids, we'd watch movies, shop, chat, or eat together. Dan loved Leticia's roast chicken and rice. When we left Ghana, I was sad to say goodbye to her, but we stayed in touch through email and Facebook. Seventeen years after we left Accra, Dan and I met up with her in Manhattan, New York City, where she was visiting one of her college-aged children. It was like no time at all had passed between us. She was still the same sweet, happy, and beautiful friend.

Ian and Ali quickly found friends at school and often spent weeknights away at their houses. Ian had a good friend whose parents worked at the American Embassy. They filled their home with American-made furniture, appliances, and all the latest toys and gadgets as the family got all sorts of perks through their governmental jobs.

"It's like the Foreign Service workers and their families still live in America," Dan often remarked after noticing how different our lifestyle was to theirs. I was even a little jealous as they could receive packages quickly and shop at the embassy store for American foods.

Ali branched out and made friends with girls who were Dutch, French, Ghanaian, and American. Since she was only in half-day kindergarten that first year, Ali came into my classroom at noon, ate her lunch, and took a nap under my desk. Both Ian and Ali started playing soccer, as that was Ghana's national sport and the primary sport taught in their physical education classes by the jovial Ghanaian teacher, known to all as Captain.

Ian also played basketball. After searching all over Accra for a basketball hoop to put up at home, Dan eventually built one himself. He bought the wood and had a carpenter cut it to the exact dimensions of a backboard, painting it green, as that was the only color found in the shops. After asking around our neighborhood, Dan found a welder, whose shop was a wooden bench on the road's side and explained how the rim would be used as a basketball hoop, giving the man the dimensions. Lastly, on a trip to the beach, Dan approached a couple of fishermen, asking to buy their net so he could use it for the hoop. After purchasing it, he could hear the fishermen laughing at the *obruni* for paying a whopping ten U.S. dollars for old netting that smelled like fish.

After Dan assembled the hoop pieces, he measured ten feet off the ground and hung it over our garage door. It was difficult to drill through thick concrete to hang it, but he did it, and the hoop never loosened or fell. Ian and Ali learned their basketball skills while playing with the neighborhood boys. When we eventually moved out of that house, Dan took the hoop down and gave it to those same Ghanaian boys.

Ghanaians revered their local soccer team and when they played at the National Stadium, Dan decided to take Ian and a friend to watch. Pandemonium occurred all around them as they hustled into the stadium. Walking into a sea of people, Dan held on tightly to the boys so he wouldn't lose them in the melee. Moving toward the seats, he could feel people pushing and rubbing up too close against him. At one point, he grabbed a man's hand just as he was about to snatch his wallet. Gunshots rang out as soon as the game ended. When the Ghanaian team lost, the angry crowd suddenly went wild. They ran onto the field, chasing the goalie into the jungle. Fearing that the mob would trample him and the boys, Dan pushed them into a ravine and lay there until the unruly crowds dispersed.

"I never heard what happened to the goalie, whether they caught him or not," Dan remarked later, "but I know it will be a long time before I attend another soccer match at the stadium."

Beach Getaway

There were many days when we went without water and electricity. Going without water was the worst for me, so if it happened on the weekend, we'd escape to the American Club. It was also our go-to place to socialize with other expat families, cool off in the pool, and indulge in hamburgers and French fries at the restaurant. Ian and Ali cavorted with their friends while Dan and I chatted with other parents. Peace Corps volunteers who got time away from their work in the villages also descended upon the Club, where they dined on cheeseburgers, French fries, and other American foods if and when they could afford them.

Dan liked to go to the Club during the American football season when they showed sports live on a giant television. We couldn't get football games at home, and because of the time difference between Wisconsin and Ghana, he'd end up waiting until midnight, then drive to the Club and watch the Green Bay Packers play. He'd arrive home at 3:00, waking me much to my distress, wanting to discuss the game. He even recruited the Ghanaian staff to become Packer fans.

Whenever we weren't at the American Club, we traveled to the beach. Bordered by the Atlantic Ocean in the south, Kokrobite Beach and its pristine white sands were well known. After asking around, Dan learned we could become members of a beach chalet that expat families used whenever they wished. Originally purchased from a local village chief years before, we just had to contribute the one-time hefty amount of twenty U.S. dollars and a yearly bottle of libation (whiskey) to the present chief, and a piece of the hut would be ours.

Anxious to get to the ocean and see our chalet for the first time, we set off on a Sunday morning with swimsuits, beach towels, and a cooler filled with drinks. The drive to the beach from Accra was close to an hour. On the way out of the city, we endured a long line of tro-tros, trucks, and cars spewing their noxious black fumes into the air.

"Roll up all the windows," Dan pleaded while turning the air conditioner on high. Breathing the air, even with all the windows up, made us sick to our stomachs.

Traveling in bumper-to-bumper traffic over the rugged roads, we exited the congested city and entered the peaceful countryside. Men, women, and children popped out on the sides of the streets selling their home-grown fruits, vegetables, and coconuts. Men dangled freshly killed grasscutters (large rat-like animals) upside down by their feet, hoping to entice drivers. After thirty minutes, Dan turned off the main thoroughfare onto a pockmarked gravel road where plumes of dust trailed our car. Driving slowly to bypass the holes, we went by men, women, and children dressed in suits and brightly colored dresses, bibles in hand as they strolled toward their church.

"Is this the right way?" I asked Dan. "I don't see any ocean at all."

"I hope so," he replied, squinting out the dust-speckled window. "There should be a village up ahead that we have to enter to get to the water."

A village encompassing a few mud houses with grass roofs and billowing palm trees came into view. Open fires cooked food in blackened pots, and women pounded fufu with long sturdy poles. Bare-breasted with babies on their laps, nursing mothers stared at our car as we bumped along. I caught glimpses of frothy waves between the coconut trees as Dan drove down a sandy hill, parking the car behind our simple one-sided chalet. Gleeful upon arriving, the kids and I jumped out onto the sand carrying our towels, chairs, bags, and cooler. We entered the hut and plopped everything down on a high wooden table partially coated with sand. The four of us stood in awe, watching as white-capped waves thrashed the shoreline. The glistening sandy beach stretched for miles both ways and a lone fishing boat bopped along in the water. There were very few people; it felt like we had the entire beach to ourselves. Ian and Ali, kicking off their flip-flops, ran towards the water, hooting, and hollering.

"Wait for me. Don't go in, yet," Dan yelled after them. "The waves look rough today." The undertow was always strong where the kids swam, and Dan never let them go into the ocean by themselves.

I stayed near the hut, preferring to sit and soak up the sun while ogling the nearby sights. Wooden boats rested on the shore while fishermen spread out their nets, repairing holes until the heat of the sun drove them away. Village kids, wearing ragged underpants, raced across the sand and dove into the surf. Ghanaian women balancing colossal pans on their heads shuffled from one end of the beach to the other, stopping to sell fresh fish and lobster. That day, I bought two lobsters and threw them into our cooler to cook later for dinner. I giggled when the woman set down her pan, and a couple of lobsters attempted to crawl up and over the slippery side. Throughout our time in Ghana, we visited Kokrobite Beach as often as we could. Leaving the city, driving into the village, and chatting with the locals always made it a venturesome trip.

A Misadventure

"I've never been so scared in all my life. I have goose bumps just thinking about it!" Dan exclaimed when he and Ian returned home from an excursion to the Presidential Palace. They set out that morning hoping to get a glimpse of the Ghanaian president's stately home. Instead, security guards with long guns stationed themselves throughout the grounds blocking anyone from getting close.

"The hairs on the back of my neck stood up, and I could feel the eyes of every guard upon us," he asserted. "The scariest part happened, though, when we got close to the entrance."

"Tell me," I demanded, color leaching from my face.

"I turned around and came face-to-face with a guard whose gun aimed directly at my head. That's when I quietly told Ian to keep his arms straight at his sides with both of his palms facing outward so that the guard wouldn't think we were about to try something."

"You're kidding!" I gasped with horror; my eyes wide open.

"We continued walking toward the entrance. The guard standing there never once took his steely gaze off of us. He stood completely still with his gun cocked. I tried to calmly explain to him that I wanted to show my son the palace. He never spoke a word, continuing to stare at us with a cold-blooded look in his eyes. That's when we turned around and walked straight back to the waiting taxi. I could still feel the gun pointing at our backs. We jumped in the taxi, and I told the driver to leave now. I couldn't stop thinking that one wrong move and we would've been dead. I know they were thinking, *I can and will shoot you if I have to.*"

Ian stood next to Dan, listening as he recounted their misadventure. "Weren't you scared?" I asked, pulling him into a big hug.

"A little," he shrugged. "There were a lot of guns pointing at us."

It'll be a good story to tell his friends, I thought to myself.

We stayed away from the palace after that, but more travel opportunities abounded in and around Ghana, and we took advantage of them.

———— • ————

Living outside the city limits of Accra had a more rural feel and was usually calm and peaceful. The loud noises in the town like cars backfiring, horns honking, dogs barking, were almost nonexistent. On most days, very little out of the ordinary occurred. The longer we lived in Ghana, the more uncomplicated and mundane our lives became. Our family felt safe. The two puppies we adopted, along with our guards, kept the snakes away. Once in a while, I heard about petty thieves, but the Ghanaians were known to chase them down and beat them, taking the law into their own hands. I assumed their actions deterred most stealing until we experienced it ourselves.

One morning, while getting ready to go to school, the neighborhood guards' whistles went off. I could hear angry voices and sandaled feet running down the dusty path in front of our house. Amidst the scuffling and cries of alarm, someone loudly shouted, *"Teef, teef!"*

"Stay here," Dan said to me. "I'm going to go see what's going on."

Dan walked outside, instantly coming upon a crowd of angry men shouting and brandishing thick sticks. The mob surrounded a thin disheveled man who carried pieces of clothing in his hands which he'd taken from other neighboring houses. They knocked him around until he was bruised and bleeding. The needy man begged, grabbing onto Dan's shirt, leaving trails of blood across his white dress shirt.

"Please, let him go," Dan pleaded with the crowd of men.

"No, this is how we deal with *teefs*. You need to stay out of it," a neighborhood guard explained with rancor.

The mob grabbed the man's arms and dragged him beyond the fields into the bush. While there, we heard they beat him and left him to suffer and die. Dan later heard that someone saw a man lying alone, bloodied, and forgotten in that area. I thought a lot about that poor man and how he must have suffered, all for a few items of clothing. *Did the man have a family*, I contemplated. *Why was he stealing clothing*? I couldn't help but wonder to myself. The entire incident would stay with me for a lifetime.

Where's the Doctor?

Waking abruptly from a sound sleep, I sat up, gasping aloud.

"Dan!" I screeched. "What's that noise? Something, or someone, is on our roof!"

"Yeah, it sure is making a lot of noise, whatever it is," Dan remarked as we lay in bed listening to the loud, rapid thumping. It sounds like some sort of animal. I better go get Isaac."

Hitting the floor with both feet, Dan pulled on his shorts and a t-shirt and went outside, yelling, "Isaac! Isaac! There's an animal on our roof. Can you go check it out?"

As Isaac climbed up the ladder, Dan asked, "What do you think it is?"

"Me, I don't know-o," Isaac replied, looking a little nervous.

"Well, be careful!" Dan shouted as Isaac stepped onto the roof.

I heard even more scrabbling and scurrying. It sounded like Isaac was wrestling with the beast. Dan watched as something large climbed down from the roof and clambered away. He came back into the house.

"It was a huge monitor lizard. Isaac took care of it." Dan explained.

Later that same morning, Ian showed me a lump on his arm.

"Mom, what's this on my arm? It's really big." Ian asked as he showed me a spot on his arm that had swelled to the size of a ping pong ball.

"Oh, God! I have no idea. Dan, come here quick," I shouted into the kitchen where he was digging into a plate of fried plantain.

"Hmm, it looks like a mango fly laid its eggs under your skin," Dan explained as he analyzed Ian's lump.

"Oh, that's disgusting!" I cringed.

"Cool!" Ian declared.

Dan applied Vaseline to the tiny hole in the center, and he and Ian waited patiently for the worm to poke its head out (I couldn't watch). When it finally started to exit the hole, Dan took tweezers and extracted the entire worm, pulling it right out of the hole.

I glanced at the worm and cringed, thinking to myself, *never a dull moment in this country.*

Whenever Dan or the kids complained of a stomach ache, headache, or some other ailment, Sarah always came up with a natural remedy. To help Dan's stomach ache, she gave him peeled ginger. She gave me lemongrass tea for my headaches and other body pains. Although ill health would hit us at times, Ian and Ali stayed remarkably healthy during those five years. However, there were occasional bouts of lice-infested scalps and amoebas that played havoc with our intestinal organs.

Soon after our arrival, teachers who'd already survived a few years in Ghana advised Dan on the different types of diarrhea that occur when a person has amoebas living inside them. They also informed us of the types of medication to take depending on the color, consistency, and odor of different diarrhea, such as the 'frothy' kind, which smelled horribly of rotten eggs.

Before we moved to Ghana, our family suffered through several inoculations. We each received vaccines for yellow fever, typhoid, hepatitis B, and hepatitis A. Ian and Ali braved every single injection without a peep. I couldn't believe what tough kids they were. On the other hand, I hated to witness my children get poked with needles repeatedly, so I left that task for Dan. We both concluded that if Ian and Ali could make it through those rounds of shots, they would be just fine living in Africa.

Despite the vaccinations, we still had to be careful of so much. Tap water had to be boiled or treated before drinking. Hanging wet clothes outside to dry was an invitation for the female *putzi* fly to lay its eggs. When the parasitic larvae hatch, it burrows beneath the wearer's skin, resulting in itchiness, severe pain, and insomnia.

Swimming or bathing in freshwater tainted with urine or stool resulted in a parasitic disease called *schistosomiasis*, or *bilharzia*. Freshwater snails released parasitic larvae, and the larvae burrow into human skin, grow, and move into various organs throughout the body, causing liver damage, bladder tumors, cancer, and even death.

Malaria, caused by mosquitoes, was frequent and as predictable as the common cold. Suffering from fever and chills, doctors often made diagnoses of malaria immediately and gave out treatment as if it were the flu. However, malaria had to be taken seriously as certain kinds, if untreated, could pass into the brain and cause death. Dan brought along the healthcare manual, *Where There is No Doctor,* by David Werner. Used by Peace Corps volunteers in remote parts of the world, he felt it would be the best medical information source. Dan read it cover-to-cover, attempting to diagnose our ailments, and sometimes, his own.

The Cape Coast

A highlight of our road trip to the city of Kumasi in southern Ghana was driving past a carpenter shop that made and sold 'fantasy coffins,' or *Abeduu Adekai*. The custom-made coffins were known to reflect the personality, status, and life of the deceased. We admired the wooden coffins carved and painted as chili peppers, fish, and airplanes. Lined up side-by-side, I viewed a casket in the shape of a man's dress shoe, a Mercedes Benz, and a Ghana Airways plane. Ghanaians believed that their dead should get the best possible send-offs and their funerals tended to be elaborate affairs, even including dancing pallbearers. The decorative coffins were parodies of the lavish funerals.

———— • ————

I had no desire to ever drive in Accra and happily let Dan do it all. The thought of getting into an accident and dealing with the police was much too frightening. The stories passed around the expat community of bribing police were enough to keep me from ever wanting to drive. Whenever we left the city, we'd pass through roadblocks set up by the military. They'd motion for Dan to stop, then slowly walk around the car, gaze into the windows, eventually asking us where we were going. Their slow, lazy attitudes and menacing stares made us somewhat uneasy, but after checking us out, they'd just wave us on.

On our way back from the Tesano Club on a Sunday, a local snooker club and swimming pool where the kids played with the neighborhood Ghanaians, and Dan and I feasted on spicy meat kebabs and Club beer, we got waved down by a police officer.

"Now, what?" Dan groaned in the car.

Pulling the car over, he rolled down his window in anger. Fed up with getting pulled over for no reason, Dan began to yell at the policeman. He knew that he hadn't done anything wrong and was determined to let the officer know it. After it became apparent that he was just looking for a bribe, Dan became even more defiant.

"Okay, I'm ready. Just take me down to the police station, and we will discuss this with the chief. I will even go to court if I have to. I didn't disobey any traffic laws, and I am not going to pay you a bribe!"

During his tirade, the kids and I sat motionless, listening but not uttering a word. *What the hell is he doing?* I thought to myself.

We have children and no way were we going to sit at a police station. Thankfully, the patrolman shrugged and, as he smiled nervously at Dan, waved us away. Screeching off down the road, I looked over at Dan noticing a pleased smirk on his face.

Driving to Cape Coast for the first time, we ran into more roadblocks handled by the military police. Again, after slowing down, Dan was waved through. Making sure we were on the correct road, though, he asked the police for directions to Cape Coast. They replied, pointing down the road, *"just there, just there."* The police often stopped tro-tros, over-filled with passengers, at the roadblocks. Gazing out at them as we passed by, I hoped they didn't have to sit on the roadside for too long as the heat of the sun was relentless.

Eighty miles from Accra, we entered Cape Coast, a city, fishing port, and a significant historical area of Ghana. Once held against their will, African men and women were confined to forts, also known as slave castles, until they boarded ships that transported them across the ocean to countries where they lived as slaves. Ghana became a republic in 1960 after surviving many years under colonial rule. During that time, slavery was an accepted social institution.

Our first excursion to Cape Coast took us along the Atlantic, where tall palm trees dotted the expansive landscape. Fishermen and women crowded the beaches as children chased each other across the sand and into the water. Flashy-colored fishing boats lined up on shore loaded down with the daily catches. Women and girls filled their head pans with fish and other sea creatures and shuffled across the sand toward the local markets.

Driving past the lively hustle and bustle of the sea coast, we could see the notorious Elmina Castle in the distance. Located eight miles from Cape Coast and looking like a white fortress high upon a hill, Elmina was once a trading post for gold and ivory. When the slave trade took over, African men and women were captured and brought to the slave castles where they were chained and their necks, wrists, and ankles shackled. The dark dungeons detained thousands of people for up to three months without water or sanitation. Forced to survive in appalling conditions, many died from illness and heat.

While visiting Elmina Castle, a tour guide walked us through the rooms with their cold, damp cement walls and floors. He showed us the dark, windowless female slave dungeons and the confinement cells for those slaves who rebelled or tried to escape. As he explained the conditions, I couldn't help but feel horrified as I wandered through the vast building, imagining the torturous agony and fear of the men and women confined to those closet-sized rooms so many years ago. The eerie appearance of markings on the walls made it even more real, sending chills through my body. Our small troop quietly and respectfully followed the guard through the '*Door of No Return*,' where, so long ago shackled men and women boarded the ships that took them far away.

We left the dark and dreary Elmina Castle, immediately assaulted by the glaring sun. Happy to be out of the gloomy and depressing building, we all felt better out in the fresh air again where we were free to come and go as we pleased. A long row of black cannons lined the edge of the castle, and I took photos of Ian and Ali standing next to them. The pictures were taken for memory's sake, as we left that day feeling there was no beauty in the history of the surroundings.

While only a few tourists visited that particular day, we knew that the slave castles were a historical attraction that often brought visitors from all over the world. In July 2009, Michelle and Barack Obama visited the Cape Coast Castle, unveiling a plaque in their honor. I assumed it to be a poignant visit for Michelle Obama, a descendant of Africans sent to America as slaves.

Driving away from the slave castles felt like leaving a burial ground. The gloomy and distressing atmosphere weighed heavily on us. In my mind, I could practically hear the shouts and cries of agony of the men and women who were locked up in those dank cells. My feelings would stay with me whenever I'd think of our visit to the Cape Coast.

———— • ————

As we headed toward the Rainforest Lodge, our mood lightened in anticipation of leafy canopy walks in Kakum National Park. Arriving at the lodge, which looked like any American motel, clean and straightforward, the kids and I waited in the car as Dan checked us in.

"We've got a room, and tomorrow morning at 9:00, we'll finally be in the rainforest," Dan exclaimed excitedly.

"Do you think we'll see lots of animals, Dad?" Ian asked, looking hopeful.

"And cool-looking birds?" Ali queried.

Listening to our excited kids, I knew I'd have to walk across the forty-meter (one-hundred thirty feet) high rope bridge, too. Peering out at it the next morning, I could already feel my stomach turn queasy. The four of us donned hard hats, and Dan and the kids crossed first. I held my breath, watching as they slowly made their way to the end, huge smiles upon their faces.

"Come on, mom, you can do it," my kids shouted as they now watched and waited for me to cross. My legs shook as I stepped on the shaky rope canopy, taking baby steps.

"Just keep walking and don't look down," Dan yelled to me. "You can do it, honey."

I continued to move forward, staring straight ahead into the misty, shadowy vegetation surrounding me. Holding on tight to the side ropes, I heard droplets of water pelt the glistening leaves and sniffed the earthy and spicy scents of wood, soil, and pine, creating an otherworldly sensation. Approaching the end, I couldn't help feeling proud of myself.

Ali ran over to hug me as I jumped off the rope ladder. "I made it!" I announced.

"You did great!" Dan said and kissed me.

Much to Ian and Ali's dismay, we didn't see any animals as most of the park species were nocturnal, but the thrashing and rustling we heard made it clear that some jungle creatures were up and about. Our trip to the Kakum National Park gave us a better perspective of the Cape Coast with its fantastic views of wildlife, beaches, glorious vistas, and rainforest, not just slave castles.

Mole National Park and Elephants

A few United States Marines deployed in Ghana showed movies on Friday nights at the Marine House. The handful of crewcut, muscle-bound marines in attendance appeared to be there for a good time, rather than keeping American citizens safe. They planned events, games, and sports nights for the American community. The Marine Ball, held each year and attended by ambassadors and U.S Embassy personnel, was one of their highlights.

The night I attended the movie *Titanic* with Leonardo DiCaprio and Kate Winslet, women filled the chairs. I was excited as I hadn't seen the film yet, and I'd heard a great deal about it. It was almost like being at an American theater and so much better than watching the pirated DVDs at home where audience members stood up and blocked the screen.

It felt great to do something fun on a Friday night, but Saturday, market day, always came too quickly. That morning Dan drove me to Osu, the business district in central Accra, and where we found a restaurant that served excellent hamburgers. We pulled into the parking lot of a well-known shop that had an assortment of American packaged foods, along with a few fresh fruits and vegetables. The shelves weren't always full, but we bought whatever we could find. After leaving the store with our purchases and walking back to our car, an elderly woman came up to me with her hand held out, *"abeg, abeg,"* she pleaded, placing her pursed fingertips near her lips. Assuming she was hungry, I pulled out a banana from my grocery bag and tried to hand it to her. She pushed it away, muttered something unintelligible, and walked off disgusted. Money was all she wanted.

Hearing a commotion as we drove out of the parking lot, I looked back toward the street and saw several young men running and shouting angrily. Some were barefoot, and others wore flip-flops, and they all waved long sticks high in the air. I suddenly felt chills down my spine as I witnessed the enraged crowd.

"Oh, no," I exclaimed to Dan. "Someone is being chased. I wonder if it's another thief." We both watched as the mob turned the corner and disappeared down the dirt road.

We drove back home with our groceries. Sarah, and her friend, Candy, met us at the door. Candy was a tailor who often sewed clothes for Ali and me with the elaborate batik cloth in vivid colors. The seams weren't always straight, and the armholes were sometimes different sizes, but I loved the vibrant colored clothing and wore it daily. The bright dresses and head-wraps that the Ghanaian women wore brought so much beauty to the country. I even put Candy's leftover cloth scraps to use as I wove them into rugs and cloth handbags on my table loom.

———— • ————

A week before our spring break, the school nurse informed me that my second-grade class had lice. She checked each child over and sent notes home to parents. Students were allowed back to school only after being treated with lice shampoo. The shampoo we needed turned out to be challenging to find in Accra. Parents who worked at the U.S. embassy tried to obtain special shampoo from their health department, but most of it had long expired. A few boys were sent back to school with their hair buzzed off, thinking that that would take care of their lice. When Ali, a student in my class, ended up with them, I corralled Sarah to wash her hair and pluck out the dead nits. All day Saturday, Ali sat on a chair in our shady front yard while Sarah combed through her long, blond hair, checking for live bugs and pulling out the dead ones. Blankets, towels, clothing, and bedding all had to be scoured before we ever felt clean again. No matter how much we cleaned, the lice scourge continued. Thankfully, the particular family that infested everyone moved to Brazil, taking their head lice with them.

Spring break came, and with it, a week's vacation from school. I only hoped that the entire lice episode would be gone and forgotten after a week away. Ian and Ali wanted to see African animals, so we decided to drive to Mole National Park near Larabanga in northern Ghana. It felt much longer than an eight-hour drive from Accra with the curvy roads and the many slow trucks. The further we got, the bumpier the drive became. Moving slowly over an infinite number of potholes, dust flying in the windows, we passed by the occasional woman and child sitting alone by the roadside, in the middle of nowhere, selling *pawpaw* or papaya. Women from nearby villages schlepped along the road with baskets of bananas or piles of wood on their heads, while small children with even tinier babies strapped to their backs ran alongside them. We encountered very few cars; however, I did notice a truck or two tipped over and lying on its side like the dead carcass of an animal, its contents long gone.

Getting out of the hectic city and touring the African savannahs' spacious landscapes always thrilled me. Large and small villages populated by round grass huts and mud dwellings with thatched roofs appeared every so often across the llano. The vistas never ceased to amaze me. Every time I saw them, I had to remind myself of where I was: Africa! *I can't believe I'm here seeing it with my own eyes.* Before our move, I only saw pictures in magazines or documentaries, but we were now living on this colossal continent with its sweltering, dry climate, unspoiled beaches, and wide-open savannahs. The appearance of its vastness always took my breath away.

Not far from the park, I noticed a group of kids striding alongside the road. I'd brought along a large bag of candies to give out, so Dan pulled to the side of the road, and I handed out a few to the children, not realizing the entire village would be watching. Dan started driving away when I looked out the back window and gasped aloud. A sizable group of children, teenagers, and women barreled towards our car. Word had spread that a car full of white people was handing out candy.

"Stop!" I yelled at Dan. "We're being chased."

"*Obruni, obruni, obruni!*" the crowd shouted as they came closer. I rolled down my window and emptied the entire contents of the bag into their outstretched hands. Dan quickly sped off; afraid the brood would want more.

An hour later, we finally arrived at the remote park, tired and hungry. Standing on stiff legs, I gazed out into the surrounding jungle, wondering how many scary animals were out there, eyeing us up for attack.

"*Akwaaba*," a park employee dressed in khaki attire greeted our family and directed us toward our bungalow. He opened the door and handed Dan the keys. The kids and I pushed through, tossing our bags onto the beds. Hungry, we walked over to the restaurant, a tiny hut filled with two rickety wooden tables and chairs. The cook had waited for us to arrive, and as soon as we sat down, four plates of rice and fried plantain were plunked down in front of us. We were starved and hurriedly ate the food; no one talked as we gobbled down our meals.

Dan and I thanked the cook for our food and promptly left. Darkness fell quickly, and it was now pitch black outside. Thankfully, Dan remembered to bring along a flashlight and shone it forward so we could find our way. I held onto the kids' hands as we stumbled toward our bungalow. The night was utterly silent, except for the eerie cries of the distant jungle animals.

Peering into the black night, Dan spotted a leopard crouching in the grass about five hundred feet from us. He whispered to me, "Jill, I think I saw a leopard right over there. I swear I saw the glare of his shiny eyes."

"Are you kidding?" I screeched in a low voice. "There are leopards here, too?"

Somewhat shaken, I followed Ian and Ali into the bungalow, leaving Dan squinting into the bush. I went to bed that night, hoping and praying the leopard would stay far away from our hut. Thankfully, we were all too dog-tired to be overly concerned.

Waking with the dazzling sun, we hurriedly got dressed. Leaving the bungalow, we trudged back to the restaurant for breakfast, rice, and fried plantain . . . again. It didn't matter as we were too excited to see the elephants that were known to roam the hills in the park. We finished eating and stepped outside to meet our elephant guide. With his trusty gun in hand and a cheek-to-cheek smile on his face, Kwame greeted us and led our eager troop of amateur elephant-trackers into the thick bush.

He led us to an area noted for spotting grazing elephants. Our group trudged uphill behind him, remaining quiet. In his broken English, Kwame warned us that if an elephant did come near and assumed the 'charge' position, we should stay on the hillock because elephants never charge uphill.

"What's the charge position, anyway?" Dan whispered to me.

It sounded safe enough, and our esteemed guide seemed to know what he was doing. We stood still and waited quietly, hoping we'd see elephants soon. All at once, two massive gray mammals lumbered forth in our direction. I glanced at Kwame, who looked off into the distance, not seeming bothered at all. When Dan noticed that the massive animal was lumbering directly toward us, his innate response to protect his family went into action. He immediately swooped up Ian and Ali and ran further up the hill, with me following close behind. Kwame, more startled by our quick getaway than because of the elephants, drew his gun. At the last minute, the scary elephant gave a loud, ferocious bellow, turned around, and slowly sauntered off, leaving Dan and me panting at the top of the mound.

"I told you that elephants wouldn't charge uphill!" Kwame repeated aloud, as he chuckled at our naivety.

The African gray elephant is the largest of the land animals, and the ones we saw at Mole National Park were no exception. I noticed that even the size of their ears was immense. Their trunks had two finger-like features, which they used to grab onto small leaves, roots, grasses, and bark.

We left Mole early the next morning, stopping at a couple of roadside kiosks along the way for snacks, water, and *Fantas*. Dan stopped once at a village not too far from the park, and I jumped out to take photos of the children. It didn't take long for more villagers to join in the pictures, smiling and huddling together as the women held their babies up and the small children waved and shouted hello.

Cape Town & Big Game

Months later, before leaving for a summer vacation in the U.S., we booked another trip for the four of us, to a game reserve in South Africa. Excited to see more animals, it would've been a shame to leave Africa without witnessing the big five in the wild - lions, leopards, elephants, buffalo, and rhinoceros. Also, anxious to see the majestic giraffes, we booked flights to Cape Town.

Flying into the airport on Cape Town's outskirts, a driver picked us up from the tour company we'd booked. Charles, an elderly white-haired South African with a lit cigarette hanging from his mouth, held open the doors to his van. We slid onto the seats and got comfortable in the air conditioning. As he drove us into the city, we stared at the zebras and *kudu* (antelope) grazing along the hillsides. Astonished to see wild animals so close to an urban area, we gazed out the windows, rubbernecking until they vanished in the distance.

After getting settled into our hotel room, the Marlboro man picked us up and gave us a Cape

Town tour. We climbed the flat-topped Table Mountain, peering out at the superb views of the city.

Charles drove us to an ostrich ranch that offered rides on the big birds. The kids were game and while they held onto the long, thin necks, I had to swat one away as it insisted on trying to peck my gold necklace off of me. We ended our day at Cape Agulhas, the southernmost tip of Africa, where the Indian Ocean and the Atlantic Ocean meet. A sign explaining the significance of the site sat upon a jagged reef where the four of us posed for a family photo. Dan picked up a rock from the mound as a remembrance and still has it today. I loved Cape Town's diversity and would've enjoyed the tour a lot more if I hadn't been nauseous from the driver's constant smoking. With the windows closed and the air-conditioning on, we still smelled like ashtrays by the time we arrived back at our hotel.

"I hope that guy doesn't drive us around anymore," I complained to Dan. "We'll all end up with lung cancer by the time our trip is over."

Thankfully, the next day a new driver picked us up, and drove us north to Sun City, a kitschy tourist resort that included restaurants, hotels, kids' play areas, and game drives. We spent the afternoons hanging out at the crowded wave pool, but the early mornings were reserved for the animal parks. Witnessing animals in the wild was the main reason for our journey to South Africa.

On the first morning, we boarded a camouflaged open-air jeep, our transportation through the Pilanesberg Game Park Reserve. While I sat in the back seat between Ian and Ali, Dan sat behind us and hung on to the sturdy bars of the jeep's roof. Before we set off, Pierre, a young, British-sounding park ranger, introduced himself as our driver for the day. He entertained us with jokes while spouting out information about the animals that roamed freely throughout the reserve. Soon into our bumpy ride, we came upon two male adolescent elephants strolling along the side of the road. Pierre swerved over to the side and stopped for a few minutes so we could get a good look at them. He let us know that we couldn't get too close as the male species tended to be aggressive.

Continuing on our tour, we spotted several hippos playing in a lake, the tops of their heads and snouts barely visible above the water. We drove by a cluster of trees, where three giraffes nibbled on leaves, stretching their necks to the very top branches. After they loped elegantly away we heard the jeep radio fizzle with static. Another driver announced over the airwaves that a pride of lions was spotted lounging together in the middle of the road.

"Hold on, everyone! We're going to visit some

lions!" Pierre shouted out as he turned the jeep around and sped off. "We want to get there before they wander off back into the bush."

The kids and I gawked at one another with anticipation. Thrilled, we huddled together, hanging tight to the sides of the jeep as we catapulted further into the park. Pierre slowed down as he spotted the pack a few yards away. He slowly moved the jeep closer so that we were directly in front of the lions. I noticed that a few hard-topped jeeps had already converged near them.

Pierre looked behind and whispered in warning, "Stay still. The slightest noise or movement could frighten one of the lions making it run toward us."

Realizing that we were in an unclosed vehicle with very little protection, I glanced back at Dan with a panicked look. Holding my breath, I watched the lions' every move. After a few minutes they seemed to get restless and when a couple of them stood up, I flinched. After one of the lions veered towards another jeep and pounced, putting its paws up on the window, Dan put his arms around Ian and Ali, warning them both to stay completely still. A few nervous seconds later, another one in the pack looked up, snapped its head around, and slowly moved toward our jeep, never once taking his eyes off of us. It was at that moment that Dan looked over at the kids and noticed Ian wiggling his fingers outside the jeep, quietly mouthing, "here kitty, kitty, kitty." Grabbing onto both kids, he threw them onto the floor and pushed them halfway under the seats. As the other drivers noticed the lions move stealthily toward us, all-out commotion broke out as rangers backed out of our way so we could leave.

It felt like forever as Pierre inched forward, then backward, then forward again, making efforts to move around the other vehicles. As he maneuvered the jeep away from the lions, I noticed him grasp onto his gun. Meanwhile, Dan kept his hands on Ian and Ali as they crouched on the floor of the backseat. When Pierre finally found a clear path out, Dan raised his voice and shouted, "Hit it!" We took off in a cloud of dust, never once looking back. After the jeep was a safe distance away, our kids crawled back onto their seats.

Dan, with his head in his hands, groaned, "I can't believe that just happened. We nearly became a lion's dinner."

The next day, a Black South African driver named Herman picked us up in Sun City and drove us back to the Cape Town International Airport. Out of nowhere, a white driver cut into our lane, narrowly avoiding our car.

"Holy cow!" Dan exclaimed. "That was a close call. It looked intentional, too."

"Yes," the driver commented in a heavy Zulu accent, staring straight ahead. "Things are not much better here. There are still too many racists."

Dan and I were surprised to hear about the ongoing racism in South Africa. We compared it to Ghana where there didn't seem to be any. Ghana felt so much safer, too.

A Presidential Visit

In August 1998, at the start of our third year in Accra, the United States Embassies in Nairobi, Kenya, and Dar es Salaam in Tanzania, were bombed. More than 200 people died. Rumors flourished that the American Embassy in Ghana could be next. With the embassy put on high alert, the Board canceled school for the next three days, and we stayed home, waiting and hoping that nothing would happen. After those three days, the staff and students returned, and the school year started, albeit later than scheduled.

Dan and I were happy teaching at the school. Ian and Ali performed well academically and had many friends. I was able to teach both of my kids when they were in the second grade, and because I wanted them to have memorable experiences, I planned creative lessons. In December, my room mother and I organized a Christmas gift-giving for a group of young children attending a crèche. Students brought their gifts to the school, and I reserved an air-conditioned bus for the trip to the nursery school. We set off in the morning, two students to a seat, holding tight to their gifts. After a forty-five-minute ride through congested Accra, the bus turned into a barren patch of land encircled with various one-story shelters. Children vied with one another as they rolled inflated tires back and forth, while women with babies tied to their backs scrutinized our group.

The students and I walked single file toward a longish cement building painted a faded yellow. Its name, Sunshine Nursery & Crèche, emblazoned across a sign hanging above the door.

"Hello!" I called, stepping through the door into a crudely decorated room, wide-eyed children staring.

"*Akwaaba! Akwaaba!*" the head-teacher welcomed us, and a chorus of sweet voices echoed her greeting.

The staff set up chairs for us, and we all sat down. The nursery children, ages two-to-seven years, sat in the room's front, effecting a small stage. We all watched, transfixed, as groups of them dressed in their finery, stood up and performed songs and dances for us. The students and I were in awe of their dancing skills and enthusiastic singing. After the final performance, we clapped loudly, and then commenced handing out the gifts. Whereas American kids would've promptly torn into the unwrapping, these children sat shyly with their presents on their laps, not touching them. They didn't understand that the package had to be unwrapped to get the toy inside. Once my students helped get them started, ripped paper and flattened bows littered the floor. Witnessing their thrilled expressions and cheek-to-cheek grins gave me so much joy. I knew the families of those children didn't have much, but I went away content and hopeful that we brought a little gaiety into their lives.

During Ian's second grade year, we built a dinosaur museum and celebrated Chinese New Year with a dragon parade. The school added new classrooms when Ali attended second grade, and her class moved into my newly-built room. It was also the year that President and First Lady Bill and Hillary Clinton visited Ghana.

Initially, rumors about their visit circulated through the American community. It was right when the U.S. and the world learned of the President's friendship with Monica Lewinsky, one of his close aides. Because of the incident, we weren't sure if the trip would be canceled or not, but in March 1998, we got word that they were coming to Accra, after all. On the morning of their arrival, Ali and a friend made a large banner welcoming the Clinton's. They wrote *Welcome President and Hillary Clinton* and wrote out their classmates' names in colorful markers. Later that day, Dan, the kids, and I, joined hundreds of Ghanaians lining the streets waiting and watching for Clinton's entourage to cruise past. We were four white faces among hundreds of Black men, women, and children. Ali and I held up the handmade banner, hoping that the President would notice it when driving past.

When the secret service cars drove by, we finally saw the President. Ali and I held tight to the banner and noticed him turn his head to look back. We were so happy it caught his attention, and later when we took the folded-up sign to the airport, he remembered and asked to sign it. I proudly displayed the banner in our classroom for the rest of the school year.

Later, in the afternoon, the American teaching staff gathered at school and rode the bus to Kotoka Airport. We stood together behind a rope that cordoned us from the podium where the Clintons would be speaking. Ian, Ali, and I had places right up in front while Dan stood off to the side, waiting to take photos.

Enchanted, we applauded for the Clintons when they finally arrived. The President and First Lady walked along our roped-off section, greeting and shaking hands with onlookers. Ian, who stood next to me, wore his Green Bay Packers football jersey, catching the President's eye.

"Who's your favorite football team?" Ian excitedly asked Clinton, who towered over the nine-year-old.

"Well, son," the President replied, putting one hand on his shoulder while Ian beamed up at him. "I'll tell you what I like about the Green Bay Packers."

Ever the politician, he praised the team and the loyal Wisconsin fans. Clinton chatted for several minutes about football while Ian grinned and nodded away. That was also the year that Green Bay won the Super Bowl. While Ian and President Clinton talked, Dan tried to jump the security lines to get photos. The Secret Service, however, interrupted him, sternly telling him to stay behind the barricade.

In a mustard-colored wide-brimmed hat and a multi-hued scarf tied around her neck, Mrs. Clinton stopped in front of me, putting out her hand. I immediately shook it and was impressed with her warmth, thrilled to be so close to her. I was, and still am, a massive fan of Hillary Clinton's knowledge, intelligence, and composure. Both Clintons were given an exuberant welcome in Accra, and their visit had been widely publicized across the world.

Doctor Dan

Always wary of contracting malaria, I made sure that Ian and Ali were in the house at dusk, the time when hordes of hungry mosquitoes attacked with malaria or dengue fever. Also, flying around at that time were colonies of fruit bats. We'd often see hundreds clustered together hanging upside in the treetops, looking like grayish lumps dangling from the branches. The bats were harmless and stayed away from us, but their sudden swoops and dives often sent us running inside.

One Monday morning, I woke a groggy Ian, who complained of a headache and chills. He also had a fever, and I told him to stay in bed. I informed Dan, who snapped up his book, *Where There is No Doctor,* and quickly opened it to the page on malaria. Believing that Ian had contracted it, Dan told me he'd stay home from school and take Ian to the doctor.

At the end of the school day, Ali and I returned home. Ian was nowhere to be found, but Dan was still pouring over the Peace Corps health manual in our bedroom.

"How's Ian?" I immediately asked.

"Oh, he's fine now, playing outside," Dan responded. "But I do need to talk to you about something quite serious.

"What is it?" I could see from the grave look on his face that he wasn't kidding.

"Well, I've been concerned lately about tingling in my fingertips. I started reading in this manual about various causes, and I'm almost positive that I've contracted . . . leprosy."

His self-diagnosis was entirely out of the blue. I knew full well that he didn't have leprosy, a disease known to affect the nerves, skin, and eyes, sometimes leading to a loss of body parts. I wanted to laugh out loud; it was just so inconceivable. He looked so scared and worried, thinking he indeed had it. Thankfully, Dan calmed down by the next morning, and never brought it up again. It later became clear that he was too preoccupied with reading about illnesses, afflictions, and tropical diseases in the Peace Corps manual, now diagnosing himself and coming up with symptoms.

———— • ————

On one of the rare occasions when Dan and I got dressed up in formal attire, we attended a fundraising dinner in honor of Dr. Jane Goodall, the world-famous primatologist and chimpanzee expert. We attended a candlelight dinner held outdoors at the Shangri-La Hotel, where a spread of delicious Ghanaian dishes covered the mile-long tables. Dr. Goodall mingled with smartly dressed ambassadors and their wives, decorated government officials, and other foreign expats throughout the night.

After dinner was over, the crowd quieted down and waited to hear Jane Goodall speak. She made her way to the microphone. In a subdued voice, she summarized her past and present work with chimpanzees. At one point in her speech, she stopped, and with all eyes upon her, began speaking in 'chimp language.' It was as though she turned into one right before our eyes; her tonality and inflections sounded so monkey-like. She made the exact guttural and high-pitched noises that chimps make when they are frightened, nervous, or just chatting with their fellow primates.

Driving home, I commented, "I wish Ian and Ali could have been here to listen to Dr. Goodall make those weird ape sounds." Dan proceeded to imitate her speaking her chimpanzee language.

Intrepid Explorers

The longer we lived in Ghana, the braver our family became, seeking out new adventures. On a trip to the western coast, near Côte d'Ivoire, we visited the Amansuri Conservation Area. Holding the largest swamp forest in the country and home to ninety-three species of birds, mammals, and reptiles is Amansuri Lake. It's also the only area that includes bamboo, mangrove, raffia palm, and coconut palm in one location. Built on stilts, the small hamlet of Nzulezo sits on the Amansuri River, and we set forth to visit it. On our way there, we traveled with guides in dugout canoes carved from actual tree trunks, called *pirogues*. Dan and Ali sat in one while Ian and I perched in another. With our river guides at the helm, we traversed the vast, murky river. I held on tight to one side, continually watching for crocodiles and hoping I wouldn't see any.

Surrounded by the dense forest, bird trills and animal calls permeated the air. The journey was peaceful until we entered a bottomless river that took us through mangrove forests. As we passed through the narrow passageway, ducking under thick, leafy branches and entangled vines, a group of exuberant village children jumped out, spooking us with their whooping and hollering. We laughed at their attempts to frighten us, waving goodbye as we continued floating along. The two guides pulled the canoes to a stop near a tall embankment in a remote part of the jungle. As they held them still, they motioned for us to climb out. We ascended the bank; I followed behind Dan and the kids as we crawled up on all fours through thickset green vegetation. After some huffing and puffing, I made it to the top, immediately crouching down to rest. Dan noticed and came over to help me back up. We continued exploring. The guides led us further into the jungle, pointing out cocoa and coffee plants and the fragrant mango and orange trees growing along the way.

Way off the beaten path, our tour group came upon a small clearing with round grass huts, smoky fire pits, and skinny goats ambling aimlessly and bleating loudly. Upon our arrival, the horned-animals scattered, and the villagers eyed us warily as they carried on with their tasks. A naked toddler took one look at us and, frightened, hid behind her mother, crying the entire time we were present.

"I wonder if they've ever seen white faces before?" I asked Dan.

"Probably not," he said. "This place is completely hidden from civilization. It's like we're explorers coming upon an ancient and remote culture."

No one spoke English, but a few of the villagers smiled at us, seemingly happy to have us visit. As a welcome, one of the younger, able-bodied men shimmied up a tall palm tree and brought down coconuts for us to eat and drink.

The four of us wandered around the grounds saying hello. The community was so small it didn't take us long to see all of it. Dan came across several men standing by a still, brewing up homemade alcohol from cane sugar. He happily accepted a cupful of the fire brew. Another group barbecued slugs behind one of the huts. Slugs, or snails, are considered a delicacy, and the four of us gawked at the villagers as they popped them into their mouths, crunching on the mollusks like they were eating popcorn. When they offered Dan one of the fat slugs to eat, he knew he couldn't refuse their courtesy. So, while the village men eagerly looked on, Dan attempted a few tiny bites, and when it was time for us to leave, the guys packed a few more for him in a 'takeaway bag.'

"What should I do with them?" he later asked me.

"Aren't you going to eat them?" I asked, snickering to myself.

"No, but I don't know if I should just throw them away," he complained.

Back at our hotel, Dan asked one of the employees if he'd like them. The guy glanced inside the bag and quickly nodded, pleased with our offer of a delicious snack.

Shopping in the Local Markets

Returning to our life in Accra, Dan found an expat teacher who wanted to sell her piano before leaving the country. He bought it, and Ali started taking lessons from Mr. Owusu, a music teacher from the University of Accra. She did well and was a dedicated student. More experienced at teaching adults, Mr. Owusu was exceptionally good with her, challenging her weekly. Her skills improved significantly under his tutelage.

As Mr. Owusu and Dan got to know each other better, they started shopping together for Ghanaian drums. Dan, a percussionist in his younger days, looked forward to practicing on the many different kinds of Ghanaian drums. He purchased a *djembe*, a rope-tuned goblet-shaped drum covered with animal skin, a talking drum shaped like an hourglass, shakers, and cowbells. He shipped them back to the U.S. with our other possessions. Dancing and drumming were popular pastimes, and events and celebrations often included drumming and dancing performances - the male and female dancers dressed in matching ethnic attire and stomped and wiggled in frantic motion.

Shopping in Accra's hot and dusty markets for handmade Ghanaian crafts was a favorite pastime of mine. Besides drums and other musical instruments, I found carved wooden masks, woven *kente* cloth, beads, handmade pottery, and vegetable-dyed baskets of all sizes. During my time in Ghana, I acquired many baskets, which caused a few heated arguments between Dan and me when it was time to pack up and leave the country. Dan couldn't understand why I needed so many, but I refused to leave any of them behind.

Strings of beaded necklaces hung in long flashy loops in the markets. In ancient times Ghanaian beads were used as currency for trading. Made of glass, clay, seeds, shells, metals, and semi-precious stones, beads continue to have great importance in Ghanaian culture. A talented woman who made richly colored necklaces, bracelets, and earrings often dropped by my house to entice me with her wares. I always found something to buy, too.

Many handicrafts and wooden furniture were handmade. Carpenters worked alongside the roads, building tables, chairs, and shelves. During one of our car trips in Accra, I noticed a chic wooden table that stood off to the side by itself. I begged Dan to pull over.

"Can we please check out that table?" I implored as he looked for a place to park. We got out of the car and walked over to take a look at it.

"This table?" he asked. "I wonder what kind of wood it is."

One of the carpenters walked over to us as we admired it. The table was tall with clawed feet and very heavy. Carved out of cherry wood, the builder explained he built it and carved the legs himself.

"I like it. Can we buy it?" I abruptly asked.

"This one's already sold-*o*, but I can make one for you in one month-*o*."

"That sounds great!" I cheered as Dan negotiated the price.

"This is the best way to shop," I told him as we hiked back to the car.

A mile down the road, sitting in patches of shade were the kente cloth weavers hunched over their looms. Multicolored woven strips dangled from a line between trees, advertising their business. Kente cloth, the traditional fabric initially worn by the Ashanti kings and queens, is woven on horizontal strip looms by the village men. With its colors and designs, each woven piece has a special meaning and represents West African culture. The three large pieces I acquired went back to the U.S. with me.

One Saturday, Letitia, my friend, and fellow teacher, invited me along to the infamous Makola Market in the heart of Accra. Never having been there before, I was amazed at the size of the place. Vendors hawked fish, fruits, and vegetables alongside sellers of used clothing, shoes, and undergarments. Crowds of people gathered along the streets, and I struggled not to get lost or bump into anyone. The stands were so close together, that while stepping precariously around a small stack of shoes, I accidentally tripped on an uneven piece of cement and fell into the display, dismantling it. Despite my profuse apology, the glowering, rotund vendor spewed a few hateful words at me in *Twi,* one of the local languages. I didn't understand what she said but heard Leticia quickly admonish her with an angry retort, which I was also at a loss to decipher, but surmised that my clumsiness had provoked the irate drama.

Bernie

Malnourished, with a round, distended belly, Bernie was just one of many homeless boys loitering on Labadie Beach. His short stature made it difficult to tell how old he was, but we assumed him to be in his late teens once he began talking to us. Bernie told us he didn't have any money and lived at the beach. I readily thought to myself, *how does he eat?*

"Well, Bernie," Dan proclaimed. "We're going to bring you to our house and give you food and a bed to sleep on."

"How does that sound to you?" I questioned. "Would you like that?"

"Okay," he shyly responded.

Earlier, a friend had told us about a boy that she often saw hanging out at the beach. She told Dan that he didn't seem to have a home or a family. So, after asking around and eventually locating him, Dan decided we should help him. That very day we took Bernie away from the sordid life he was living at the beach. He moved into our home and soon started calling me "ma." I didn't mind, feeling rather pleased to have someone else call me that. He seemed to need mothering, too.

Bernie had a bedroom in our compound. Ian offered him clothes that he no longer wore, and we invited him to eat, play, and watch T.V. with us. He soon felt comfortable and happily chatted with everyone, especially Dan, who he insisted on following around. Bernie stayed with Sarah and Peter while we were at school, but it didn't take him long to find his way to the tall school gates. He began to show up there daily, asking for Dan and interrupting his classes.

We wanted to help Bernie improve his health and bought him the recommended medicines. Dan asked around and found a carpenter who agreed to employ Bernie and teach him a trade to make money and live independently. His life seemed to improve as he got healthier and learned new skills, but one day, he up and left without a word after living with us for several months. Much later, we learned that Bernie had passed away. Because he had suffered prolonged malnourishment for so long, his organs entirely shut down. We helped pay for a respectful and decent burial for Bernie, as he had no one else who could help him.

My wish to adopt again lingered in my heart. When we moved to Ghana, I had hoped to pursue it. Chloe was gone from us, and we missed her terribly. After giving ourselves time to grieve, I had hoped that we would find a child that needed a family and a home. The poor and homeless children we saw were a harsh reality. Dan and I felt that we had so much to offer a child, and we were ready to bring another one into our family.

Our attempts at adoption took us to various government offices in and around Accra's business district. We visited the U.S. Embassy, inquiring about adoption under U.S. immigration laws. Dan and I visited the Ghanaian Adoption Authority and the Department of Social Welfare, even bringing whiskey bottles and boxes of cookies for bribes. *That's how to get things done in Ghana;* people apprised us.

That November, after a long wait, we finally heard back from the agency. One of the female advocates made an appointment with us for a home study. It happened to be Thanksgiving on the day she arrived, but despite coming down with a case of malaria, the agent carried on asking us questions and examining our house. Sarah was in charge and spent all morning cooking our Thanksgiving feast. She cooked turkey, stuffing, and mashed potatoes for the first time. Thankful for our feast, we invited the woman to stay and enjoy a real Thanksgiving dinner with us. *How could she possibly not accept us as adoptive parents,* I thought as we plied her with pumpkin pie and whipped cream. After eating a plate full, she thanked us and left, informing Dan and me we'd hear from her. However, we never did, and when we went back to the agency to inquire about our status, they informed us we'd have a better chance of adopting if we were European. Dan was ready to give up, although I wasn't. I made an appointment with a lawyer, but when he said he'd travel to one of the villages and offer to buy a baby for us, we left dumbfounded. It was something neither of us would've even considered.

Our school year was also winding down, and we planned on leaving Ghana soon. Just when I was ready to admit that it wasn't going to happen, a young American woman approached us while we ate lunch at the American Club. She informed us that she was a missionary and knew a pregnant woman with her fifth child. The woman had no husband or means to support another child. *Could this be the opportunity we waited so long for?* I sought out Dan with raised eyes. Trying to contain my excitement, I told her we'd gladly take the baby as our own. Sadly, once again, it wasn't to be. The village woman gave birth to a stillborn baby girl. Instead of supporting and caring for a new baby as we thought, we gave her money to pay for hospital expenses, a funeral, and food to feed the rest of her family.

Good Bye Ghana

The year 2000 and the Y2K scare provoked havoc around the world. Unsure what would happen concerning airline computer systems and other electronics, we went back to the U.S. for a four-week Christmas break. It turned out that all of the commotion about the world ending wasn't true, so we flew back to Ghana at the end of January.

Although the internet came to the country in August 1995, our school didn't have computers until 2000. The first fast-food restaurant also showed up in Osu that year. It served hamburgers and fries but wasn't at all fast. Accra was changing, and our life there was also coming to an end. Five movers came to our house that June, packed our belongings in boxes, and loaded them onto a colossal truck to be shipped by boat to our home in the U.S. Every item fit in the semi-truck, baskets, drums, wooden furniture, a five-foot wooden giraffe, even the wicker furniture that I begged Dan not to leave behind. I wanted to bring back every Ghanaian souvenir and memory that I collected during the five years.

It was an emotional time for me on that final

day. Saying goodbye to Sarah, Peter, Isaac, and Candy, who'd become part of our family, walloped me. I broke down the minute I noticed them lined up together to see us off. With heavy hearts, Dan and I hugged each one. I cried many tears, knowing I'd never see any of them again. Later that afternoon, we gathered with school colleagues one more time at a hotel pool. While there, I shed more tears as I hugged Leticia, wishing her and her family well. The goodbyes were tearful, but we looked ahead to our future, ready for more travel opportunities. In June 2000 our family left Ghana for good. We returned to the U.S. for another summer vacation before flying to Guadalajara, Mexico, to take on our next teaching assignments.

On our last trip from West Africa to the United States, we flew through Europe and stopped for a few days in Rome, Italy. The time there helped to take our minds off of everything and everyone we left behind in Ghana. While in Rome, we saw it all - the Colosseum, St. Peter's Square, the Pantheon, and the Trevi Fountain. We toured most of the city on foot and our kids, now ten and eleven years old, hung with us the entire time.

On a few occasions, however, we opted for the train. On one of those train trips, we encountered young pickpockets, as they mentioned in our guidebooks. While standing together in the aisle watching for our stop, six teenaged boys and girls inched closer to Dan. Looking like the tourist he was, the teenagers zeroed in on his bulky purple fanny pack, which practically sang out, 'come and steal me!' Dan's fanny pack contained all of our passports, identification, and money, and once he realized they targeted him, he shouted out, "Watch out! These kids are trying to rob us! They are pickpockets!" None of the passengers reacted to Dan's shouts. I figured it was because most Italians were used to seeing thieves on trains.

"I don't think anyone is going to help us. Let's get off at the next stop," Dan said, clearly upset that no one seemed remotely interested in our predicament. The riders almost looked bored with the entire scenario.

When the train stopped, I led the kids out the door, wanting to get away from the thieving group. However, they all got off, too, and began to follow us. We continued walking ahead while the teenagers kept moving closer to Dan. He quickly took his backpack off and waved it around as if swatting at swarms of bees.

"Get away from me, you little-----! Leave us alone!"

The group finally left when they noticed the Italian Polizia walking over. That incident didn›t spoil our love for Rome or Italy, and we happily visited several more times.

PART 4 – GUADALAJARA, MEXICO

2000-2001

Buenos Días
("Good Morning" in Spanish)

No Hablo Español

We arrived at the Appleton International Airport to learn from the agent that no planes would be flying that day. A powerful electric storm had hit Wisconsin, lighting up the sky with violent flashes, so we turned around and started for home. With the weather looking better the next day, we set off to the airport again. Dragging our bags up to the checkout counter, Dan waited for his turn.

"Sorry, but you are two-hundred-fifty pounds over the limit. That will cost you three thousand dollars extra," the American Airlines agent declared, a tight smile on his face.

Dan, eyes wide in shock, swiveled his head toward me. I looked away, glanced at the ceiling, at the floor, anywhere but at his fuming face. I stood back and cowered in the corner, letting him deal with the agent's request.

"But we called the airline earlier. I told them about our oversized luggage, and the person I talked to said we would only need to pay two hundred dollars extra. Why are you telling us something different? Can you call someone?" he pleaded.

Several agonizing minutes passed as we watched the ticket agent type furiously on the computer keys. Finally, she agreed to reduce the astronomical fee and let us board the plane, oversized bags, and all. Breathing a sigh of relief, Dan thanked her. I gathered up my carry-on bag, gave her a weak smile, and mumbled my thanks. Before entering the plane, Dan caught up with me.

Through gritted teeth, he spat out, "I'm sick and tired of hauling your shoes, clothes, purses, books, and everything else across the world! When is this finally going to end?"

———— • ————

In August 2000, we flew to Guadalajara, Mexico, our fourth country and the third continent in nine years. After the flight delay, the over-priced cost of our bulging suitcases, and Dan's displeasure, we weren't off to a good start. Moving is always stressful, but traveling across the world with all of our belongings had started to take its toll. It now felt more tiresome than adventurous. That June, we had moved back from West Africa. A semi-truck arrived a month later filled with our furnishings. After getting settled and unpacked, two months later, we were off again.

Despite Dan's desire to stop traveling and stay in Wisconsin, I believed we still had one more country to conquer, and I wanted it to be Mexico. I even hoped that it could be a place to retire to someday, a long way off. I begged Dan and eventually wore him down. While finishing up our contract in Ghana, we contacted the American School of Guadalajara, interviewed, and the director hired us over the internet. With access to computers by that time, Dan and I could contact schools, research teacher vacancies, and scan campus photos. Since 1991, we'd traveled the globe without access to the internet or cell phones. Besides trolling for schools, we could now communicate with friends and family wherever they were.

Teachers working in international schools today can't begin to realize how difficult it was when airmail and expensive long-distance phone calls were the only means of communicating with others thousands of miles away. Sending, or receiving mail, took weeks, sometimes months. Christmas packages mailed before December never reached us until March or April. With the newfound online network, we now could email, bank online, and make our plane reservations. Working overseas had become more manageable, and the world felt smaller.

Cucarachas (Cockroaches)

As we planned our next move, I pictured in my mind just what kind of house I wanted in Guadalajara. I dreamed of a quaint Spanish-style bungalow with a red tile roof and a lovely terrace with tropical flowers, cacti, and lush, leafy ferns. I corresponded months before we moved, arranging with a couple to take over their place. It had a garden, two stories, three bedrooms, and furnishings. From the pictures they sent me, it looked perfect. However, I soon found out otherwise, and my dream house never materialized.

We arrived at the Miguel Hidalgo Y Costilla Airport at night. A short flight, but still exhausting, we met a woman from the school business office and her boyfriend. I immediately got the feeling someone had bribed them into picking us up as their welcome wasn't very enthusiastic. The couple drove us to our new *casa* (house), handed over the keys, and after we retrieved our luggage from their car, sped off down the street. Dan opened the front door, and I stepped inside, followed by Ian and Ali. The sight of umpteen fat, brown cockroaches lying belly-up on the floors, like brown smudges on the white tiles, sent me reeling.

"Keep your shoes on!" I shrieked at Dan and the kids. I didn't want them to touch the floors with their bare feet until I swept, mopped, and disinfected every inch of that cockroach-infested floor. The grossly fat insects lay on the floor exactly where they took their last breaths. The crackling sound their shells made when stepped on, and the way they wiggled their tiny legs and antennae while lying helplessly flat on their backs, creeped me out. Give me the lizards or geckos of Africa any time, but not cockroaches. Once I realized that cockroaches were part of everyday life in Mexico, I tried to ignore them, but always had the exterminator's phone number on speed dial.

I'd thought our move to Guadalajara would be effortless and a pragmatic move for our family. Flights to and from Wisconsin were shorter; we could even drive a car there in thirty-three hours. No more would we have to endure the long, grueling, twenty-four-hour flights across the world. It felt good to be in the same hemisphere and time zone as our family back in the U.S. We wouldn't have to wake up at two o'clock in the morning to phone home, either. We could continue to live the overseas life and revel in another culture, despite being closer to the United States.

The second-largest city in Mexico, Guadalajara, is three-hundred-fifty miles west of Mexico City. It is known widely for its tequila and mariachi bands that roam the streets. Large parks, historic areas with charming buildings and plazas, and cathedrals populated the city, giving it a Hispanic vibe. Still, the shopping malls, fast food restaurants, and large grocery stores filled with Mexican and American brands made it feel like a U.S. city. We could find and purchase just about everything we needed, a massive change from our life in Ghana, where we went without so many American amenities. Happily for us, a supermarket called the *Mercado Gigante* was located just a few blocks from our house. Dan happily volunteered to do the week's shopping there after learning the salesgirls handed out free samples of tequila to all the shoppers.

———— • ————

Peculiar to us was the sight of armed soldiers standing at attention in front of banks, stores, and gas stations. With their long guns slung casually over their shoulders, they glared, unsmiling at anyone that came close.

"Don't stare," Dan admonished Ian and Ali whenever we passed them.

Their appearance was slightly unnerving to us the first morning we ventured out to look for our school. We heard it was nearby, and Dan and I wanted to see it and show the kids. However, walking the streets and trying to locate the American school was impossible. We needed to ask for directions, but after approaching at least three people to help us, we gave up and trekked back home. No one spoke English, and Spanish was still incomprehensible to us.

Teacher orientation began the week before school started, and Ian, a sixth-grader, and Ali, now in fifth grade, tagged along with us on those days. I felt sorry for them not knowing anyone and already bored. The overseas teachers were from the U.S., Canada, and Guadalajara and tended to be young and single, coming to Mexico to learn Spanish and travel the country. There tended to be a party-like atmosphere among the young teachers with drinking and socializing on the weekends. Once again, the fact that we had kids, and now our ages, made us feel at a disadvantage.

The students, primarily Hispanic, came from wealthier families. Rumors of a few drug-dealing parents also circulated. I taught a class of twenty-five first graders during the first half of every day, while the Spanish teacher instructed them in the afternoon. My students were lovely, and their parents were supportive. Even the young first-graders spoke English and Spanish fluently.

Ali and Ian entered middle school as the minority *Norte Americanos* with their blond hair and green eyes. They stood out among the other predominantly dark-haired middle schoolers. Luckily, being a bilingual school, they could converse with the other students in English and quickly made friends. They also had a daily Spanish class together, and both picked up the language quickly.

Walking home from school with Ali one day, I took a chance and stopped at a *panadería* (bakery). The woman behind the counter welcomed us, and I pointed to the pastries that I wanted; thankful I didn't have to speak any Spanish.

"*¿Algo más?*" she asked me, and I suddenly became flustered, not understanding her.

"*Sí,*" I answered with a smile but said nothing more. The salesclerk and Ali stared at me for a couple of seconds as if I was unhinged.

"Mom, she's asking if you want anything else," Ali whispered to me.

"Oh . . . no," I quickly answered, embarrassed but immensely proud of my daughter for her Spanish abilities.

Lost in Translation

"I know that I relayed my order correctly this time! They are messing with me and giving me the wrong food on purpose because I'm a *gringo*!" Dan stated furiously.

After going through the drive-thru at McDonald's, Dan received the wrong order again. We soon relied on Ian and Ali to translate for us. Thanks to the intensive language classes and conversations with classmates, they got better and better. Dan and I had our Spanish class once a week but spoke English the rest of the time. We were not picking it up as quickly as we'd hoped. While living overseas, I wanted Ian and Ali to learn another language, and Spanish seemed to be the most suitable. Most of the students I taught overseas spoke two or three languages, and I had visions of our kids also becoming bilingual.

———— • ————

I continued to put off getting a haircut because of my limited language skills. But I gathered up my courage one Saturday and walked into the *Salón de Belleza* (hair salon) that sat at the end of our street. Without a photo and using my limited Spanish, I explained to the stylist that I needed a trim. The stylist seemed to understand, nodded a couple of times, and began to cut. When she finished, I looked in the mirror and gasped, noticing she'd cut quite a bit, much more than I'd wanted. Somewhere in my translation, she must have heard "cut it all off."

"What happened to your hair?" Dan asked me when I got home.

"I asked for a trim, at least that's what I thought," I told him before rushing upstairs to the mirror to try and fix it.

Haircuts in other countries were always stressful for me. I never knew how I'd end up looking, but that one was the worst.

Learning the language would become our biggest hurdle. Most of the people outside our school community seemed to speak only Spanish, so we knew we'd have to learn quickly. Communicating with salespeople to order cell phones, install the internet, and set up all of the utilities in our names turned out to be incredibly infuriating. Even ordering bottled water for the first time proved to be an impossible task. When I caught sight of a truck delivering water bottles on our street, I shouted to Dan.

"Hurry up. I see the water truck parked across

the street. Let's go ask the driver to deliver our water," I said.

"Okay, let's see if we can do this," Dan replied, looking somewhat unsure.

"Maybe he'll speak some English," I wished aloud.

We ran outside, hoping to catch the driver before he left our street. We soon learned that he didn't speak any English, so the two of us tried communicating with him using hand signals, miming, and whatever we could think of. It took at least twenty minutes to relay to him that we wanted bottled water delivered to our house. Thankfully, a neighbor, and one of the teachers at our new school, observed our dilemma and translated for us.

———— • ————

Along with Spanish, we had tutoring in the Mexican culture and traditions. The Day of the Dead, or *Día de los Muertos*, a multi-day holiday, was celebrated all over Mexico during November. The Spanish teacher assembled an altar, *ofrenda,* in my classroom with flowers and pictures of the students' dead family members. I thought it a bit morbid at first, but then understood that the holiday symbolized love and respect for their deceased. The celebration of life and death included colorful sugar skulls, *Pan de Muerto* or Bread of the Dead, and *papel picado,* pierced papers that held symbolic meaning during the two-day festivities. Parades took place in some parts of Mexico, and obligatory visits to cemeteries where relatives placed marigolds on gravesites.

Sofia, the Dog

The first day of school began in August, right before Ali celebrated her ninth birthday. That month typically found us on a plane flying back to some country, or looking forward to relocating to a new house and school. Our family always celebrated her birthday with a cake, but without friends or extended family, and often in a hurry. As teachers, we were constantly preparing for a new school year around that time. However, that year Dan wanted to do something special for Ali. She had wanted a dog, but it was never the right time. Without friends and family nearby to help celebrate, the guilt weighed heavily on us. Dan wanted to finally get her a pet so she'd have a memorable birthday.

Once Dan told Ali they would find her a dog, there was no stopping them.

"Where are you going to go?" I asked him.

"I'm not sure, but we'll find one," he said, smiling, putting his arm around her.

"Well, okay, but make sure you bring back a dog that isn't too big and doesn't shed!" I shouted after them as they walked out to the car. Shaking my head, I watched them drive off into the city where Dan didn't know his way around or speak Spanish.

Hours later, much to my surprise, the two of them showed up with a six-week-old yellow Labrador puppy. Not only would it grow to be large, but labs were also one of the worst-shedding dogs. Ali's rambunctious puppy bounded through the front door, jumped up and licked each of us on the face in greeting, knocked over vases of flowers with her tail, and made a puddle of pee on the dining room floor. She then bounded up the stairs to the bedrooms with Ali close behind her.

"Couldn't you have asked for a smaller and calmer dog?" I whined to Dan.

"I did, but Ali wanted this one," he stated.

"Does she shed much?" I asked next.

"Well, the guy said she doesn't. At least that's what I thought he said, but he only spoke Spanish, so I'm not exactly sure," Dan sighed.

"I guess we'll wait and see," I grumbled to myself.

Ali and her dog, which we named Sofia, were constant companions. She grew to be a feisty, mischievous, and much-loved member of our family, even though she loved to jump on people and dig holes in our garden. Dan and Ali found a dog park near our home, and the first time they drove there with Sofia, she zeroed in on a street cat and flew headfirst out of the window. Notorious for running away from home, Sofia seemed always to know when the gate latch was open. There were many times when we had to scour the neighborhood, calling her name. On one day in particular, while I stood in front of our house looking fixedly up and down the street, a strange car drove up.

"Is this your dog?" A woman asked me as she leaned out the window. Trailing next to her car was Sofia, tail wagging back and forth, happy to be home again. Dan and I were sure that she understood Spanish, or there were many times she would've stayed lost.

Sofia also proved to be our fearless protector. Early one morning, Dan woke to hear loud and continuous barking. Afraid we might be getting robbed he jumped out of bed and hurried downstairs. The wild barking came from the kitchen where Sofia had trapped a black scorpion in the corner. As soon as Dan noticed it, he picked up a cast-iron frying pan and swung it, killing the scorpion. Patting Sofia on the head, he praised her for protecting our family.

———— • ————

That November, we went off to Cancun, a resort city in the Caribbean. We had to leave Sofia behind and asked neighbors to come by and feed her, returning to an ecstatic puppy, but a yard in complete disarray. Miles of hotels, white-sand beaches, shopping centers, and restaurants made up the tourist city. We stayed at one of the posh hotels where my mother and niece also joined us. A tour bus took us to the Mayan Ruins of Tulum, a highlight of the trip, where we climbed the massive number of steps to get up to the castle and the cliffs' stunning views.

Later, while on a boat trip to Xcaret Park in Playa del Carmen, I sat with my mother up on the top level. However, once the waves got too rough, tossing us around like we were inside a washing machine, our nausea came on quickly. A crew member escorted my mother to the bottom level, and I followed close behind. Thankfully, we both made it to the end of the trip without vomiting. That day the kids swam with the dolphins, the highlight of their vacation, and Dan got in as many dives as he could. After recovering from seasickness, mom and I shopped at the craft markets.

———— • ————

Back at school, Ian joined the middle school basketball team and made forays into skateboarding and surfing. A typical teenager, he played his music too loud and had his first girlfriend. Ali had an American group of friends who got together for birthdays and had sleepovers at each other's houses. Whenever they came to our house, Sofia stayed with them, making sure the girls included her. She'd lie with them curling her body next to the girls as they laughed and talked into the night.

Ali continued to take piano lessons after Dan bought her an electric piano. She joined the drama club and made her stage debut in the musical *West Side Story.* Cast as Anybody's, the tomboy. She performed for four straight nights. Dan also joined the cast as Officer Krupke, the nightstick-wielding policeman who kept order between rival gangs.

Each night I watched him repeat his only line, "Knock it off! Settle down!" while holding onto a doughnut. I sat in the first row through every performance, snapping photos of him and Ali, clapping proudly. Less than thrilled with being cast as the doughnut-eating, pot-bellied policeman, Officer Dan was glad to see the performance come to an end. He endured it all for Ali, though.

Home and Back Again

The holidays came, and with them the end of our first semester at the American school. Amidst the celebrations, red and green decorations, and the blooming of pink poinsettias outside homes, the four of us flew back on a one-way ticket to Wisconsin for Christmas. Dan and I discussed taking a road trip back to Guadalajara instead of flying. We decided we were up for the adventure, so after a week home in the snow, Dan and I loaded up our 1978 Jeep Cherokee and drove it across the U.S. into Mexico with our two teenagers in tow.

"Are we all ready for this long trip?" Dan asked as he got behind the wheel. His parents watched from the window as we waved goodbye and set off.

An interminable journey, we were thankful not to have to endure snowstorms or slippery roads. We drove into Missouri and through St. Louis, gazing up at the Gateway Arch, which is the tallest human-made structure in the western hemisphere. Stopping for two nights in hotels, we mostly ate on the road. The kids and I shed our sweaters and parkas as the weather got warmer the further south we headed. Finally, after a little over two days, we arrived in Ciudad Juarez, the border town on the Rio Grande, south of El Paso, Texas.

"I'm going to stop at the Walmart here," Dan said as he drove into the vast parking lot filled with pickup trucks and minivans.

"Why? What for?" anxious to cross the border, I wanted to keep going.

"I've got to buy a steering lock, so our car is safe in Mexico," Dan replied as he opened his door. "The teachers warned me that carjacking occurs all of the time there."

While inside Walmart, Dan left us and walked quickly to the automotive center. I stood and scanned the store, bewildered. The layout was the same as the Walmart in Wisconsin; however, the signs were all written in Spanish, and everyone around me spoke it. It felt a little surreal. Dan reappeared with a sturdy lock while I grabbed two bags of spicy nacho chips, handing them off to him at the checkout counter. After making our purchases, we left the store and jumped back inside the car. Dan tried out his new apparatus, showing me how it attached itself to the steering wheel.

"This should do the trick," he said, looking pleased with the gadget.

"Okay. By the way, did you hear that our Spanish teacher's car had been stolen right before Christmas?" I asked him, confident our car would now be safe from would-be carjackers.

Dan consulted the map again before driving out of the lot. Finally ready to cross the border into Mexico, I scanned each road sign that we passed. Despite our conclusion that we were on the correct route, we suddenly found ourselves on a remote path leading to nowhere. Dan careened through a ravine, then hot-footed onto a vacant dirt road, and lurched up onto a paved side road. The route took us entirely by surprise, and the roadway appeared utterly deserted, with no houses or shops. Neither did we see any automobiles or people, but we motored on.

"Where are we?" I glanced at Dan, crouched over the steering wheel, staring hard at the road in front of him. "How did we miss the road for the border?"

"I'm not sure," Dan remarked, scratching his head.

"Are we in Mexico yet, dad?" Ian asked, peering out of the windows.

"I think we are, Ian. I just don't know exactly where in Mexico," Dan answered, incredulous that he bypassed the Bridge of the Americas and the U.S. border. As we continued driving into northern Mexico, I kept glancing out the Jeep windows waiting for the Mexican or United States customs agents, with sirens wailing, to catch up with us. Instead, no sirens blared, and our entire drive seemed eerily quiet. The only vehicles we passed were rusty pickup trucks overloaded with people and animals. It almost felt like we entered Mexico through the back door.

The scenery changed the further we advanced into the country. Barren landscapes, desert cacti, and blowing tumbleweeds gave way to fast-food restaurants and *taquerias*. Seventeen and half hours later, tired and hungry, we approached the historic city of Guanajuato. The fascinating metropolis captivated us with its colonial pink and green sandstone architecture, narrow, winding roads, and street tunnels extending beneath the city.

Dan parked the car, and we found a hotel for the night. Ian asked to see the *Museo de las Momias* or mummy museum, and since it was nearby, we strolled over. The museum held more than one-hundred bodies of men, women, and children from the nineteenth and twentieth centuries. The mummies were interred naturally in glass cases; some with their mouths open as if screaming in pain, and others clutching their arms, hugging themselves. There were mummies still with strands of hair and wearing pieces of their original clothing. Babies and 'the world's smallest mummy' were also on display. We had been unprepared for the dark and morbid place and its many gruesome sights of shriveled bodies, and we left before reaching the end.

"That was cool!" Ian remarked while the rest of us sat in the sun and gulped fresh air, forcing the visions of those desiccated fossils from our minds.

With only a three-hour drive ahead of us, we were back on the road early the following day. All thoughts of dried-up mummies were gone. We cruised the smooth highway, arriving in Guadalajara around noon.

"Yay!" Ian, Ali, and I shouted when we drove under the sign, *Bienvenidos a Guadalajara,* welcome to Guadalajara.

"We made it!" Dan pronounced, clasping my hand tightly.

Sure we'd be home in no time, our journey through Guadalajara with its myriad streets and traffic circles proved utterly confusing. Although we had lived in the city for a few months, it was our first time driving through it. After taking wrong turns, turning onto dead ends, and going the wrong way on one-ways, we were all sick and tired of being in the car. Dan's frustration had reached its limit. After two hours of driving around Guadalajara's complex maze, we finally found our house, arriving spent and relieved.

———•———

Our days of walking to and from school were over. I'd miss strolling past the homeless woman who sat on her tattered blanket selling homemade toys, with her two children next to her. I never bought anything, but Dan always dropped a few *centavos* into her cup to help her out. I wouldn't miss crossing the busy street in front of the school, however. It was a matter of life and death as drivers disregarded the red light and 'walk' sign, even if pedestrians were standing in the crosswalk. Walkers did not have the right-of-way on that street, and drivers had no patience to wait for them to cross.

Once, after waiting on the corner for the walk sign to flash, I looked both ways, and stepped off the curb. A driver turned the corner and nearly ran me down as he hit the gas pedal like a competitor in the Indy 500. Only an inch away from my right hip, I stopped and yelped. Oblivious, he drove off, but not before I pounded my fists on his trunk and screamed obscenities at his recklessness. Furious with the insane drivers, we never let our kids cross without us, too afraid they'd get hit.

———— • ————

I liked to walk in the different middle-class neighborhoods and look longingly at various charming Spanish-style homes in bright colors. Dan and I imagined ourselves buying one with a private terrace filled with terra-cotta pots full of yellow frangipani flowers and tall cacti. However, what often started as peaceful strolls ended in a frenzy of howling from the 'roof dogs.' Dogs throughout Guadalajara were placed on the tops of houses and businesses in the early evenings, acting as security alarms. They stayed up there all night long, attempting to scare away intruders with their persistent yapping. Since the dogs couldn't get down from the roofs, barking was all they could do to keep the homes safe. Keeping dogs on the tops of buildings, I found out, was a low-budget security system for Mexicans and illegal, but that didn't stop the practice.

Diving with the Humpbacks

Soon after school started again, Dan enrolled Ian and Ali into diving classes. He'd received his certification years ago and wanted both kids to learn. They attended six weeks of lessons at a nearby recreation center pool. Once they completed the training, their dive instructor scheduled both of them for their first underwater test. Our trip to the ocean took us through the hills and mountains of Western Mexico toward Puerto Vallarta, a seaside resort town on the Pacific Coast.

Driving along the wide-open highways with the windows open and our hair blowing in the breeze, felt invigorating. We loved taking road trips through Mexico and planned to take even more. Despite the many stops to pay the expensive tolls, we entertained ourselves by singing along and bobbing our heads to the beat of Smash Mouth's song, *Walking On The Sun*, an appropriate tune as the scintillating sun glared in the dazzling sky, not a cloud in sight.

We cruised by the popular high-end hotels that lined the streets and made our way to the town center. The hotel we booked ahead of time advertised itself as charming, quiet, and well-located, but the air conditioning didn't work, and roosters crowed loudly outside our window. The views of the ocean from the boardwalk that ran along the ocean, however, were impressive.

Up early the following day, Dan, Ian, and Ali were excited about finally getting into the ocean. I followed them to the dive shop, where they gathered their equipment. Hanging onto towels and water bottles, I followed along as the divers carried their wetsuits and air tanks, trudging along together toward the waiting boat.

"Time to hit the water!" Dan quipped as he waved to the crew already lingering on the boat.

A forty-five-minute cruise by speedboat took us to the middle of the ocean. The craft stopped, and the divers began their preparations. I watched Ali pull on her wetsuit and fins and observed Ian check his pressure gauge and buoyancy compensator. When they were both suited-up with their air tanks and mouthpieces attached, masks covering their faces, I snapped a few photos to remember the moment. I couldn't help but become emotional, though. My two babies were about to dive deep down into the dark recesses of the Pacific Ocean, where I wouldn't be able to set eyes on them for several excruciating minutes. I wasn't much of a swimmer, and the thought of diving underwater petrified me, but Dan assured me they'd be okay.

"I will stay near both of them the entire time. If anything goes wrong, I'll bring them up to the surface right away," Dan explained, trying to put me at ease.

The three of them looked like professional divers sitting on the edge of the boat with all of their gear. Their backs facing the water, they each gave me a little wave, and I blew them a kiss. With a loud splash, one by one, they fell backward, plunging into the deep water. I peered over the boat, holding my breath as tears streamed down my face. The gurgling bubbles soon fell silent as they dropped further beneath the surface.

I remained on the boat with two other crew members, waiting for Dan and the kids to resurface. While I stood staring out across the ocean, attempting to balance myself in the teetering vessel, out of nowhere, two colossal whales shot out of the water and into the air like erupting volcanoes. A mere fifteen yards away, a mother humpback and her baby crashed through the waves, and then slammed back down into the ocean. Gasping in utter shock, I looked over at the guys who laughed and pointed. Shocked, I continued staring out at the spot where I saw the whales, hoping the divers would come up soon and the humpbacks would return; otherwise, they'd probably never believe me.

A few minutes later, Dan and the kids returned to the surface. As soon as I saw them come up, I shouted, "WHALES! I just saw WHALES!"

Dan yelled out, "Where?"

And with perfect timing, the two giant humpbacks soared once again out of the water, into the air. The divers hooted and hollered with excitement. We saw the mother and her baby jump through the water a couple more times before continuing on their journey into parts unknown. Ian and Ali passed their dive test, earning their certifications, and we all got to witness humpback whales up close in the Pacific Ocean.

———— • ————

Many international teachers will agree that one of the benefits of working in overseas schools is the lengthy vacations written into the school calendars. The long holidays made it easy for parents to take their families on long vacations and enabled teachers to take advantage of travel opportunities. We crossed a great deal of Mexico during our year in Guadalajara; it seemed like we were there more to travel than to teach.

On one of our extended weekends, we journeyed through the forested hills into the state of Michoacan. The cool fresh air surrounded us as we neared the village of Angangueo, the winter home for Monarch butterflies. Four hours west of Mexico City, at ten-thousand feet, the tiny hamlet lies amongst a misty fir tree forest within a valley surrounded by mountains and terraced fields. Our Jeep with Dan at the helm, climbed the hills along curvy roads where steep hillsides and jaw-dropping views made me gasp in fear. By the time we arrived, Ian, Ali, and I were moaning with agonizing bouts of car sickness from the constant up and down motion and swerving along narrow, curvy roads.

I noticed signs that read, *Cuida a la Mariposa* (careful with the butterflies). The smell of smoke from the burning wood stoves permeated the air as women dressed in colorful hand-woven shawls, cooked *tamales* and tortillas for the tourists on their way to view the butterflies.

Dan found a parking space and stopped the car. After exiting my seat I stood, shaking out my stiff legs. "I don't see any butterflies," I announced after looking around.

"Well, according to this sign, we have to walk up a hill to see the place where they congregate," Dan informed me as I groaned to myself. "At least, we'll get to stretch our legs," he added.

Our troop of butterfly explorers found the entrance and trudged up the trails, tromping further up the steep hill. Forty minutes later and out of breath, we reached the narrow path at the very top. Standing together in awe, amidst the quiet stillness and reverent calmness, we gazed at thousands of butterflies clinging tightly to the tree bark, nestled against the cold morning air. They looked like they were sleeping with their wings tightly closed, but once the sun peeked out from behind the clouds, the butterflies slowly awakened. Their wings opened and fluttered, sounding like a gentle rain falling. The four of us assembled on tree logs, quietly watching as the Monarchs hovered nearby, occasionally settling on us as softly as reticent kisses.

One Long Road Trip through Mexico

Mexico, a profoundly Catholic country, celebrates *Semana Santa* (Holy Week) the week before Easter. Businesses close for a few days, and schools let out for the week. The week is also a popular time for families and teachers to head out to the overcrowded beaches.

Dan planned and mapped out a family excursion for us along the west coast, stopping in several small Mexican towns along the way. We had eight days to enjoy our Mexican tour, taking us through the Pacific coast's fishing villages, then back up through Oaxaca and Mexico City, back to Guadalajara. With Dan, the driver, me, the navigator, and Ian and Ali as passengers, we set off. Taxco, a colonial hill town known for its *plata,* silver jewelry, became our first stop. The town's cobblestone streets led to an abundance of silver jewelry shops. I was instantly overwhelmed by the plethora of silver baubles in each one. Glass shelves overstocked with shiny silver earrings, bracelets, and necklaces made me almost giddy. So much to look at and try on, I couldn't choose and left empty-handed.

"Don't worry," Dan teased. "There will be plenty more items to buy. Your shopping trip has just begun."

From Taxco, we continued to Zihuatanejo, 'place of women.' Cruise ships stopped here, and tourists visited *El Centro* with its brick-lined beachfront promenade. The well-known *playas*, or beaches, gave me a chance to sunbathe while Dan and the kids snorkeled. We left Zihuatanejo early the following day so that we could get to Acapulco before noon. Halfway there, however, the police stopped us. Two villages were engaged in a brawl, and we needed to turn around or wait until the villagers reconciled. Hungry for lunch anyway, we stopped and pulled over near a local cafe to wait out the disagreement. While there, Dan and I chatted with other expats, biding our time until it was safe to drive. They gave us tips on places to stay and good restaurants to check out on our trip down the coastline. Three hours later, the discord had ended, and saying *adiós,* we got back into our car.

Acapulco, another seaside town backed by the Sierra Madre del Sur Mountains, gained its popularity in the 1950s for its glitz and glamor. Known as the resort for Hollywood jet setters, Frank Sinatra and Liz Taylor were among its frequent visitors. When we visited in 2000, however, Acapulco had lost its shine. The beaches were not as pristine as others along the coast, and the hotels were shabby and rundown. With the trash-filled streets, ever-present drug dealers, and prostitutes lurking, just walking to the corner drugstore felt risky. Acapulco didn't feel very family-friendly, and we moved on again the following day.

We stopped to catch glimpses of the *Clavadistas de la Quebrada,* cliff divers, outside of the city. As we stood on the viewing balcony, our eyes settled on four divers, pausing at the edge of a one-hundred-thirty-six-foot high cliff. Before they jumped, the *clavadistas* prayed near a makeshift altar of the Virgin of Guadalupe, set up on the cliff. Once the tides brought forth the tallest waves, they gauged when to jump, wowing us with a series of spins and flips then straightened their arms and dove straight into the deep, churning ocean. Awestruck, I remembered seeing the divers on a television show, but catching them in person was even more miraculous. We left our viewing post to continue the drive south.

Two hundred miles down the seacoast, we reached the surfer town and fishing hamlet of Puerto Escondido. Surrounded by coffee *fincas* or farms, the port town had a laid-back atmosphere where dread-locked hippies lounged and sold tie-dyed clothing from small wooden shops. Sauntering through on the way to the beach, whiffs of marijuana smoke accosted my nose. The white-sand beaches were pristine, and *palapas,* palm-covered shades looking like umbrellas, dotted the expansive oceanfront.

I noticed the surfers and boogie-boarders skimming the waves as I found a spot to sit on the sand. Dan immediately rented a couple of boards and took Ian and Ali out to the water. Fifteen minutes later and already starting to burn, I looked up to see Ian and Ali running toward me, Dan slowly following behind. He plopped down onto the blanket and laid there for five minutes, panting heavily.

"Are you okay?" I asked, touching his head.

He rolled over to face me and, in a weak voice, uttered softly, "I felt so afraid and helpless. The undertow was unbelievably strong. I fought it, but it took all of my energy. I thought that we were going to be dragged out into the middle of the ocean."

"If we wouldn't have been on the boards and had just been swimming, we would've been carried out into the deep," he stated in a shaky voice.

I could tell Dan had indeed been afraid, which surprised me as he is a solid and experienced swimmer. That extreme terror of getting caught up in a vicious undertow never left him; he still remembers the fear today.

Puerto Angel, the final coastal town on our journey, popped up like a guidebook photo.

Already alive with families celebrating Good Friday, hills scattered with papaya trees and bougainvillea surrounded the blissful bay. Ordinarily peaceful, Mexicans from all over now converged onto the small fishing port for the *Semana Santa* festivities. Dan pulled into a hotel, and Ali and I jumped out, joining the procession already moving slowly up the hills. While the man playing Jesus carried a large wooden cross up the narrow trails, the procession stopped periodically to pray aloud, and then continued onto the next location. Ali and I made it halfway, but as the sun rose higher in the sky and the heat enveloped us, we left to join the guys at the beachfront.

Ready to move on from beach towns, we drove east into the hills. The scenery became more rugged as we drove past wooden hillside shacks with tin roofs. Squawking chickens, braying donkeys and frisky goats meandered through the neglected yards, and wooden roadside stands sold coffee, bananas, and honey. I looked forward to arriving in Oaxaca, our next stop - an authentic and charming colonial Mexican city where indigenous rug weavers, potters, and wood-carvers plied their skills.

"Won't this be exciting?" I asked Dan, grabbing his arm, causing him to swerve, nearly hitting some manic chickens.

"Oh, yeah. I can't wait to shop some more," he groaned in a less than enthusiastic tone.

Besides being a shopper's paradise, Oaxaca happens to be the culinary capital of Mexico. Restaurants there served up various *mole* sauces, dark gravy containing a variety of spices, and chocolate. After arriving in the city and eating our spicy chicken mole and rice meal, we wandered over to the central plaza. Sitting on a bench, we listened to a *Mariachi* band perform its heart-wrenching ballads and watched hammocks-sellers peddle their colorful string cots, the impressive Cathedral of our Lady of Assumption off in the distance.

After a week of driving from one Mexican town to another, we were all tired. Dan was anxious to head back toward Guadalajara. Finally able to shop in the markets, I left Oaxaca with pottery, hand-woven wool rugs, vibrant *huipiles,* traditional dresses, and embroidered blouses. As we packed up and Dan carried my purchases to the jeep, he grunted and groaned, making room. Giving me one of those looks, he finally found space, shoving it all in.

"The only reason you like to travel is so you can shop. You believe that the world is just one big shopping mall," I grimaced at Dan's accusatory tone.

I do love to shop, especially for one-of-a-kind handmade artifacts from other countries. The bartering that goes with it is also part of the fun. It also felt good knowing I'd be helping to support native women and their families through their handmade art.

Mexico City, our next destination, proved to be a nightmare. Quite the intricate maze, the traffic jams, one-way streets, and useless maps made it even harder to find our way through the metropolis. Thankfully, Ian and Ali slept and didn't hear Dan mutter obscenities as he maneuvered us slowly through the city. We got lost a few times but did see parts of the city that we otherwise wouldn't have. Once on the right track, we made it back to Guadalajara, weary but intact.

Homeward Bound

Two months left before the end of the school year. Dan and I had to decide if we wanted to stay for another year or move back to Wisconsin. We discussed the pros and cons and ultimately decided the time had come for Ian and Ali to experience life in the United States. We left Wisconsin in July 1991 and lived and traveled the world for ten years until 2001. During that time, the four of us visited twenty-five countries, giving us memories for a lifetime. Our family gained so much—Ian and Ali learned patience as we dealt with difficulties, respect for cultures different than their own, and they made a host of new friends from around the world. They both learned Spanish and acquired better geography skills than most American kids their age.

Dan purchased a trailer to transport our clothing and household items to Wisconsin. However, after learning we needed a special permit to pull a trailer into the U.S., he returned it, losing out on the six-hundred dollars he originally paid. Having to develop a new plan, I left Dan that final morning pondering the situation, gripping a handful of ropes and bungee cords in his hands.

"The Jeep will be packed and ready to go by the time you come back," he shouted to me as I walked toward school and my classroom for the last time.

Back at the American school, I packed and put away another elementary classroom. The halls were already empty of students and teachers who had left for summer vacation. I picked up my final check, hugging the business manager, whom I hardly knew, in a moment of wistfulness. Arriving home, Dan stood outside the car, sweating, still digging out space for our last few items. The car top was piled high, numerous ropes holding everything in place. I glanced inside to see boxes and crates stacked so tightly together I was afraid they might fuse in the oppressive heat.

"Are you sure there'll be enough room inside the car for all of us?" I asked Dan.

Sofia surprised us and jumped into the front passenger seat, curling up into a furry ball. She refused to move and spent a lot of the morning lying there. Sofia knew we were leaving and didn't want to be left behind. After a great deal of pushing and prodding, we ejected her from the front seat, moving her to the back. The kids and I settled in the car while Dan jerked one more time on the ropes, making sure everything stayed in place. Feeling good about his packing, he jumped into the driver's seat and started the car. Sofia stuck her head out the window and stayed that way through the entire drive north. We backed out of the driveway onto the street, and our three-thousand-mile cross-country journey began.

¡Hasta luego Guadalajara! ¡Vámanos!

PART 5 – REVERSE CULTURE SHOCK

2001-2007

Hey, What's Up!
("Hello" in Wisconsin Slang)

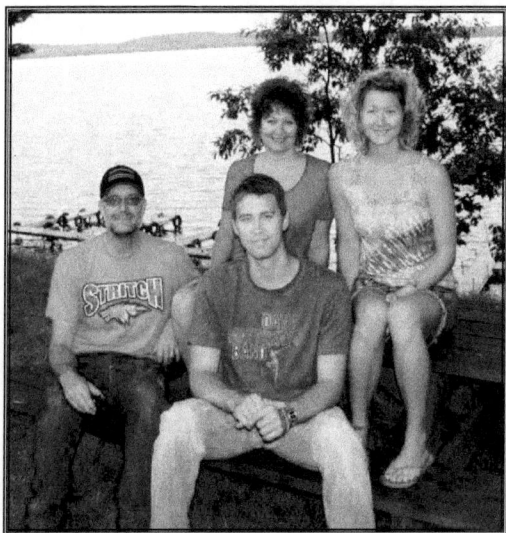

Dan, Jill, Ali, and Ian Dobbe
Wisconsin, USA - 2010

Homeward Bound

"Are we there yet?" Ali asked in a muffled voice, pushing Sofia's butt away from her face. For the three thousand miles of driving, Ali patiently endured Sofia's fifty-pound body lying across her lap, making for a very long, hot, and uncomfortable trip.

"Not quite, but I think we're going to make it," Dan replied as we crossed the Illinois-Wisconsin border, the last leg of our journey.

Thank God, I thought to myself, beyond sick and tired of the drive. We were all more than ready to exit the Jeep, no one more than Dan, the lone navigator for three days, a staggering twelve hours of driving per day. The end was near, and he focused on making it to Wisconsin before nightfall. For the last five hours, no one even dared to ask to use the bathroom for fear it would spoil Dan's steely determination to get us home before dark.

We arrived in our hometown on the 4th of July and tooted the horn three times to announce our arrival. Pulling into my in-laws' yard, we came to a final and complete stop. The back door flung open, and Sofia bounded out of the car, rolling around on the grassy lawn, as happy as all of us to be back in Wisconsin. The rest of us slowly unfolded our stiff legs from the confined seats, stepped out onto the ground, shaking and stretching every part of our bodies that hadn't gone numb. We were relieved to be back home again.

———•———

Our first few weeks home felt surreal as we adapted to being back in Wisconsin. The sensory overload was overwhelming. Grocery stores and shopping centers were prominent— cars, newer and shinier. Yards were green, well-maintained, and as large as football fields. Everything appeared clean, with roadsides free of plastic bags and other debris. No horrible urine or sewage smells accosted our noses in the warm summer air. Tap water was safe to drink, and the plumbing worked, drivers followed road rules, we no longer had to wait days or weeks to have our utilities turned on, roads were smooth with no potholes, and businesses stayed open the hours they advertised. Police officers toting high-powered guns no longer were present on street corners. Life, back in the U.S., seemed so different, more manageable, almost enchanting.

The interests of the general population took us some time to get used to, however. Twangy country music had taken over radio airwaves. The craze for reality television popped up, and the new show, *Survivor,* seemed to be a big hit. The large meal portions at restaurants garnered our astonishment. *My breakfast order at IHOP could have easily fed a family of four,* I thought to myself. Dan and Ian attended a baseball game that summer. When the game paused during the 7th inning stretch, and music streamed loudly from the speakers, fans shot out of their seats and performed the Macarena dance in sync. Everyone in the stands, minus Ian and Dan who were oblivious, got into the dance movements.

I visited the grocery store soon after we arrived in our hometown. The extra-wide aisles and neatly arranged shelves were in sharp contrast to the cramped and empty markets I'd shopped at overseas. Delighted and amused by the abundance and variety of meats, loaves of bread, seafood, pastries, and packaged foods all in one place, I also found it somewhat daunting. The task of choosing which foods to purchase became too much for me. I hunkered down for twenty minutes in the cereal aisle alone, baffled by the many different brands. The longer I gazed at the boxes, the more helpless and agitated I became. Dizzy from the enormous array of foods, I gave up that day and walked out of the store, shaking my head and mumbling to myself like a crazy woman.

Thankfully, I could now get a decent haircut with a stylist who could understand my needs. Dan didn't have to worry while we lived overseas. He never swayed from his usual buzz cut and looked forward to the neck and back massages, always part of his haircut routine. On the other hand, I suffered every time I went to the salon. Besides African women, Singaporeans and Latinas were blessed with long, smooth, straight locks, while I showed up with shorter, wavier, and finer hair.

A barrage of feelings engulfed me during those first weeks—excitement and happiness—but also disorientation and resentment. My feelings bounced around like ping pong balls. One day I felt content being back in the U.S., and the next day, disconcerted. I didn't feel ready to give up traveling, and I already missed the thrill and adventure when living in a foreign land. I found it difficult to even talk about our travels. No one seemed interested in hearing our stories of being the only white people in an African village or balancing on a rope ladder hundreds of feet above the rainforest. We found that most often, our friends and family hadn't ever heard of the places we traveled to, nor could they find them on a world map.

While overseas, we had become comfortable living with like-minded expats who, like us, had a more global outlook. They tended to be less selfish, more open to multiple viewpoints, and appreciative of different ways to experience life. In our small, conservative community, the attitudes and perspectives toward other cultures and races were less open-minded. At times, I felt offended by the cultural stereotypes that still existed.

Reverse culture shock was a reality, and Dan and I experienced many of the feelings that our friends overseas warned us about . . . "Life in the U.S. isn't going to be the same for you anymore. You will be lonely and will feel like you have nothing in common with anyone. You'll feel misunderstood, and people won't get why you left the U.S. in the first place." Our colleagues proclaimed we'd have trouble adjusting to the faster pace of life, so redolent of American culture. We heeded their warnings, and they were correct.

"Everyone is so white here! And they all speak English," Ian exclaimed during his first visit to the shopping mall.

Now, teenagers Ali and Ian were also experiencing reverse culture shock. During the past years, they'd lived with brown and black-skinned Asians, Africans, and Latinos. They had lived with people from other races for so long that they became used to being the only foreigners, or 'white kids.' Their blond hair and white skin were now the norms in Wisconsin; they no longer stood out. However, the two of them were distinct in other ways. The soccer skills that Ian picked up in Africa and Mexico weren't sought after in Wisconsin, as soccer wasn't a popular sport. He missed out on learning to play the more popular Wisconsin sports of football and baseball. Ian's new friends were also hunters, a sport unfamiliar to him. The music popular with their schoolmates was also alien to both. They had to quickly catch up by learning the band names and their popular songs.

Used to living a more sheltered life overseas, we had to get accustomed to giving Ian and Ali more independence. No longer were we acquainted with their friends or their parents. Teenagers held parties on weekends where they smoked and drank, with or without parents in attendance. Despite having more freedom, Dan and I continued to involve ourselves in their lives, proudly watching their basketball games, get dressed for the prom, earn their driver's licenses, graduate from high school, and go on to college.

———— • ————

When I look back at everything we saw and what we accomplished during those ten years abroad, I can happily say I'd do it all again.

Despite the cultural faux pas, the language barriers, and the lengthy plane rides, it was all worth it. Dan and I often felt like the oddballs taking our two small children abroad when other teachers were either young and single or already retired. Still, their enthusiasm and curiosity brought us continual joy.

"How did you and dad do it?" my daughter, who now travels with an eighteen-month-old, once asked me.

"You and Ian were a big part of our adventures," I replied. "We couldn't have done it without you."

Afterword

Since writing and publishing the first edition of this book, our family dynamics have changed.

Ian graduated from college and went on to medical school. He married and now works as a doctor in Alaska. An avid fly fisherman, Ian still loves to travel as long as he can take his fishing rods along with him.

After Ali graduated from college, she moved to Honduras and now teaches Biology and Computer Science in the International Baccalaureate Program. She met her husband, also an expat teacher, and together they gave us our first grandchild.

During our six years back in Wisconsin, Dan and I earned our Masters in Educational Leadership. We returned overseas, working in Cairo, Egypt, Gurgaon, India, and Tegucigalpa, Honduras, where we continue working as school administrators.

No longer traveling with kids, Dan and I adopted a Yorkie-Poo named Mickey, who now travels everywhere with us. When we are not traveling to Alaska to visit Ian, the two of us enjoy touring Central and South America with our dog in tow.

Acknowledgments

Thank you . . .

Shannon and team at Orange Hat Publishing/ Ten16 Press. You gave me the help and the confidence I needed to turn my story into a memoir. It was your quirky name that got me, but it is your genuine warmth and supportive emails that will make me forever grateful.

Tracy and Nigel, for your excellent editing skills and for keeping with my preference for American translations.

Ian, for reading my long forgotten journal and for reminding me that I had some good stories in it. Your support now and always means everything to me.

Ali, for being the first to actually read my writing and to find it amusing. All your suggestions were right on and they encouraged me to keep going.

Betty, my mother and shopping partner, for all the help and time you gave in managing our affairs in Wisconsin while we were overseas. It is still difficult to say goodbye to you every August, but it is always truly a joy to return and see you again.

Dan, for accompanying us, leading the way, and for carrying our kids and me across the world and back. You helped to give us many stories and then put the idea in my head to actually write a book about them. Thank you for that, and most of all, for giving me your undivided love and support, so that I am able to live a life true to me.

About the Author

Jill Dobbe is an international educator, travel writer, amateur photographer, and author of three travel memoirs. She makes her homes in Tegucigalpa, Honduras, and Wisconsin, USA, along with her husband, Dan, who continues to complain about carrying too much luggage.